China Dreams

Singular Lives:
The Iowa Series in
North American Autobiography
ALBERT E. STONE,
SERIES EDITOR

China Dreams

Growing Up Jewish in Tientsin

By Isabelle Maynard

Foreword by Albert E. Stone

University of Iowa Press Ψ Iowa City

University of Iowa Press

Iowa City 52242

Copyright © 1996

by the University of Iowa Press

All rights reserved

Printed in the United States of America

Design by Karen Copp

Many of the names in this book have been changed to
protect the privacy of the people portrayed.

Printed on acid-free paper

Library of Congress Cataloging-in-Publication Data

Maynard, Isabelle, 1929–
China dreams: growing up Jewish in Tientsin / by Isabelle
Maynard.
p.   cm.—(Singular lives)
ISBN 0-87745-562-7 (cloth), ISBN 0-87745-571-6 (paper)
1. Jews—China—Tientsin—Biography.   2. Tientsin
(China)—Biography.   I. Title.   II. Series.
DS135.C5M39   1996
951′.154004924′00922—DC20
[B]   96-24321
CIP

01 00 99 98 97 96 C 5 4 3 2 1
01 00 99 98 97 96 P 5 4 3 2 1

To my parents,

SOPHIE AND DAVID ZIMMERMAN,

with love and admiration

Contents

Foreword

ALBERT E. STONE

WHO, MANY READERS of *China Dreams* may legitimately ask, is Isabelle Maynard? What entitles her to publish an autobiography that reads more like a collection of short stories than a conventional confession or memoir? Given a combination of relative authorial obscurity and manifest mastery of the language of memory and emotion, this author of a haunting narrative of girlhood takes her place among contemporary American autobiographers, including her thirteen predecessors in Singular Lives: The Iowa Series in North American Autobiography. She will, I predict, secure a sympathetic reception from a range of readers: coterie and general, adult and adolescent, female and male, Jewish and Asian American. None, I suspect, will catch her in a single pigeonhole; all will feel the affinities.

Like many autobiographers today, Isabelle Maynard is a first-time book author. Like many, too, she has ample experience to tap and translate into unique literary form. Born March 3, 1929, in Tientsin, North China, she now lives in Emeryville, California. After a succession of careers—as actress (of stage, radio, film, and television), painter, teacher, writer (in drama, short fiction, verse), social worker, and most recently, oral historian—she has become the consummate talented Northern Californian, fully at home in the multicultural, multimedia environment of San Francisco. Through the changes and challenges of her Pacific world she carries a distinctive identity as personal and cultural achievement. "I think of myself as a person who is perpetually astonished. Also a watcher of people, conversations, and landscape." This mature self-characterization also fits the young girl who came of age on the coast of China five or six decades ago.

The astonished observer arrived at consciousness of self and society in pre–World War II Tientsin. She was the only child of Russian Jewish

ix

parents caught in this teeming city on the North China Sea without passports. The family faced impecunious statelessness in a chaotic world rife
with revolution, war, refugees fleeing both, and implacable anti-Semitism.
From Tientsin Isabelle at last escaped in 1948 to California. Only a few
final chapters—vignettes, really—describe the first experiences of her and
her parents in San Francisco. The bulk of the narrative, set in Tientsin,
records a growing girl's perceptions and responses to a crowded household
with its melange of parents and other relatives, older Jewish boarders, one
DP (displaced person), and silent, often nameless Chinese servants. From
this center (which was neither home nor womb), the narrator moved into
the city's crowded streets, beaches, and parks, as well as schools for foreigners, convents, clubs, a hospital (once), and a movie theater. This rigorously segregated and separate city included Europeans (and a few Americans) who held economic and social power and were surrounded by a large
Chinese population. The foreigners—English, French, Germans, Italians,
Americans, and Russian—insolently ignored the Chinese, keeping themselves apart in "concessions," or treaty-port enclaves. Within and between
these distinct worlds (timeless, apparently, for the Chinese, temporary for
all others) lived the Jews. "We were there not by choice," Isabelle recalls,
"but by circumstances of history, remnants of the Russian Revolution, and
we diligently suppressed in our own minds the fact that we were in a foreign land by accentuating the internal ties of the community. We had our
own school, our own club, our own organizations and businesses. As Russian Jews in China we were thrice aliens."

Out of such ironic perceptions and feelings of a lost time and world
Isabelle Maynard has composed an arresting life story. "I left China in
1948," she remembers. "I returned for a visit in 1981 and came back completely flooded by memories of my childhood. The only way I could deal
with them was to write about them. I then realized I was writing about a
community no longer in existence, which further propelled me into sharing these memories with others. . . . I mull things in my head, and when
I feel I am about to explode internally—I write."

Though this conflicted author is more Americanized and less traumatized
by Russia or the Holocaust than some other refugee writers, her confes-

sions reveal emotional affinities and literary strategies linking her to well-known émigrés and rememberers. Two of the most famous, who, like her, combine fiction with autobiography and deploy astringent and nostalgic imaginations upon doubly lost worlds, are Isaac Bashevis Singer and Vladimir Nabokov.

The phrase "more Americanized" undercuts, I hope, the rather grandiose comparison of this writer with the authors of *In My Father's Court* and *Speak, Memory*. Isabelle's Tientsin lacks the depth and breadth of both Singer's Warsaw ghetto and Nabokov's aristocratic Vyra. More plausible as parallels to *China Dreams* are several more recently published coming-of-age stories by native-born Americans, which capitalize on similar childhood situations and anxieties such as deracination and marginality, fallible parents and other uncomfortable adults, awkward awareness of one's body, nascent sexuality, and, above all, high-test childish imaginations. On these adolescent themes Frank Conroy wrote *Stop-time* and Maya Angelou began her autobiographical sequence with *I Know Why the Caged Bird Sings*—as did Maxine Hong Kingston, very differently, in *The Woman Warrior*. Even older autobiographers of girlhood like Lillian Hellman and Mary McCarthy have published memorable works that combine memoir and fantasy. To be sure, Isabelle Maynard mentions none of these books or authors in her text. To have done so, perhaps, would have anchored her too firmly in an American cultural context quite different from the one the young girl actually experienced in thirties China—Hollywood movies, old *Vogue* magazines, Montgomery Ward catalogs.

More important to Maynard than looking backward through clear American eyes is depicting her former self looking forward to America as a shadowy goal at the end of a cloudy girlhood. Hence dreams and dreaming are central metaphors of the self and of others. The principal dreamer was, of course, Isabelle. Despite (indeed, because of) the often gritty realities of her suspended existence, she developed an interior world made of "solid ground and fluffy clouds." Like other Europeans, she ignored the Chinese almost entirely, calling even her faithful nursemaid simply "Amah." Yet in one of Isabelle's nightmares Amah murdered Buddy, the family's incontinent puppy. Many other dreams, though escapes from boredom, were filled with dread. Her parents' noisy nightmare quarrels; the

silent and furtive friendship of Braverman the DP; her friendship with an
older Englishwoman who opened the world of books; the casually cruel
anti-Semitism of Russian Orthodox and American Embassy playmates;
self-assured schoolmates who agonized less than she over physical appearance and popularity—each actual situation was grist for a sensitive girl's
reworking into something closer to reverie.

Though nearly all foreigners were also dreamers, Isabelle's father was
her chief model. "Because he always dreamt out loud, my father was my
choicest childhood companion. . . . I developed into a watchful child, as
dreamy and imaginative as my father." Indeed, the family's capacity to
dream away reality became fine-tuned. Anti-Semitic slights, dwindling
funds and hopes of escape, brutal Japanese soldiers, even Isabelle's first
menstruation (which the dictionary politely taught her to call "menarche") were unpleasantries that the father in particular was able to ignore,
never speak about, dream of alternatives to, escape from in books. The
family's sacred code of silence covered (or sought to) all disagreeablenesses.
Even Isabelle's mother, the practical and active partner and guide, bowed
to the iron rule of wordless ignoring. "You have to learn to accommodate,
to put up with certain things. You'll understand when you're older."
Balancing these two models of deportment while usually favoring the father became the task of this girl's first writing experiments, as in this
oblique entry in her diary that treats a crisis at school precipitated by ugly
anti-Semitic words daubed on the wall, a fight between Russian and
Jewish youths, and her first menstruation:

> I wrote in my diary later that day: "Saw 27 today. He was quite a hero, but
> probably never will really see me. There were huge yellow words on the wall
> at school. Bad words. Had my first red spot. This has been a day of colors.
> Red and yellow make orange. It has been an important day. May 24, 1942."

"Everyone pretended nothing had happened" may, indeed, describe many
remembered moments of this exotic girlhood. The terse sentence comes at
the end of *China Dreams*'s most dramatic episode. It is in fact Isabelle's
most heroic hour. Her beloved Aunt Mary had, to the consternation of
the entire community, married a Russian Orthodox *goy*, Walter Denko.
At an anniversary party, Walter got monumentally and pugnaciously
drunk. In a rage he shouted suddenly, "'Get out of my way. I want to sing

alone. . . . More vodka,' he yelled. 'More. More. More. To mother Russia. Down with the Yids.'" In the stunned silence that followed, little Isabelle "got up and walked toward Walter. He towered above me. 'You unwanted horrid fiend.' My words seared my tongue like hot coals, filling my chest cavity until I felt I would explode. 'You unwanted hideous fiend.' Walter looked like a deflated balloon, all saggy. Tears rolled down his cheeks."

As this electric episode suggests, the dreamy schoolgirl, like the mature author, sometimes became a seething cauldron of feeling. Yet her sense of irony never deserts the writer, who may, of course, have embellished the scene. Isabelle Maynard is frank enough to round out her heroine's outburst thus: "I felt utterly exhausted and stretched out on the maroon couch, ignored by the guests and my family. It was as if my rage had dropped like a stone to the bottom of a deep pond without even a ripple left to show its existence."

Isabelle isn't the only family star in this otherwise unheroic narrative. As prelude to the last, bleak chapter on the family's first months in San Francisco comes "The Hero of April 8–9." This, the longest chapter in *China Dreams*, is likewise the only one without young Isabelle present to tie past and present together. Instead, it recounts (as told by him) the father's escape from Tientsin six months after the departure of wife and daughter. "He did not perform a striking feat of courage or save anyone against great odds, nor was he magnificently noble in a desperate act. During those two days, he stood still and allowed himself to flow with events around him." Nonetheless, his nighttime escape was, at least in his daughter's retelling, breathtaking. Although "timid, emotional, easily frightened, romantic, scared of doctors and dentists," he managed to respond to chance and opportunity (furthered by the Swiss Embassy, the Red Cross, business bribes, and a faithful rickshaw coolie) to reach the side of a British cargo ship in the bay. "Well, Yid, up to freedom," the drunken stevedore shouted. Then the mousy man crept up the ship's swaying ladder, "drenched with fear and the desire to succeed and egged on by the jibes below."

The family's reunion in America has little of the drama and even more of the irony displayed by the hero of April 8–9. Now a young woman, Isabelle returns to center stage as the family's financial mainstay and hope. Her narrative concludes on a bitter note. Little of the fabled beauty and

freedom of San Francisco survives as the fresh immigrants struggle through
a series of depressing jobs.

> My mother gets up to bring more soup. The stuffed cabbage rolls sizzle
> gently in their juice behind me on the stove. From the hallway we hear
> Mrs. Bosak's muffled voice making connections to our future.
>   "Salute! To the Promised Land!" my father says, lifting his cup of
> orange juice.
>   We join the toast. "To the Promised Land."

Readers of American women's autobiography who recall the upbeat
treatment of Mary Antin's Americanization in *The Promised Land*, published in 1912, will understand best the bittersweet finale to this female im-
migrant's coming of age in a later America.

Acknowledgments

THIS BOOK WAS a journey through my past. Many people along the way sparked my imagination, kindled ideas, and ignited memories. But *China Dreams* would never have been born as a completed book without the encouragement and support of Peter Tripp, who goaded and urged me to completion. I appreciate his nurturance and faith in me even when I was ready to give up and the many hours he spent with me in planning this book.

I acknowledge with much gratitude the gentle and wise, well-thought-out criticisms offered to me by Marcy Alancraig and Katie McBain during the last seven years and their staunch belief in my capacity as a writer.

I also send a thank you to Marilyn Nottingham for her patience and her impeccable skills on the computer.

Prologue

THE DREAMS THAT are the genesis of this collection of stories began when I was nineteen years old and was forced to flee Tientsin, China, with my parents. Though new to me, refugee status was already familiar to them, as they had escaped the Russian Communist Revolution years earlier. They had stopped in China, planning only to stay a short while before emigrating to America. But since no one else wanted stateless Jews in their country, their short stay stretched into twenty-five years.

In Tientsin, my mother and father joined a large number of other Jews trapped in China. Looking back, I realize that the way they suppressed their sense of not belonging was to organize their own universe within this exotic foreign land. By the time I was born, we Jews had our own school, our own social club, our own synagogue, and our own businesses.

Though it wasn't obvious to me at the time, it is clear now that we were, by circumstances of history, thrice alienated. We were alienated from the Russian community; we were snubbed in China by the more prosperous and self-proclaimed high-status Americans, English, Germans, and French, who were not only more financially secure but—more important—had passports from a country they could return to. We had only booklets stamped "State-less." And last, we alienated ourselves from the Chinese people by choice, snubbing them as we ourselves had been snubbed. Perched precariously on this foreign soil, we put down no roots, bought no homes, and seldom learned the Chinese language. I never had, I'm sad to admit, a Chinese friend while I was growing up, only servants that I was much too good at giving orders to. The closest I came to a friendship was with Amah, my Chinese nanny who cooked, cleaned, and picked up my clothes from wherever they lay. I never called her by her real name, only by "amah," the Chinese term for servant. This is what I had been taught; I knew no other way.

In 1941, after years of paperwork and disappointment, the door to America creaked open, and we were finally approved for emigration, only to have our dreams ruined by the Japanese attack and occupation of China. The open door clanked shut. Trapped now more than ever, we could only wait for the end of the war and the American soldiers to free us, trying to survive as refugees in a now occupied and hostile land. Liberation from the Japanese came with the end of the war in 1945, but American rules and regulations had changed and the endless emigration process resumed.

In 1948, when I was nineteen, my parents and I left this land that had sheltered us for many years and fled to America. The Communists were approaching, and we were becoming personae non gratae. It was my parents' second flight from Communist revolution, prompting my father to wonder, "How many revolutions does a man have to endure before he enters the promised land and is free?"

Not until I was living in the safety of America did I realize that the land where I was born and raised would now be as inaccessible to me as Russia was to my father. It was then that the dreams began. Tientsin dreams of growing up; of joys and sorrows; of boyfriends and girlfriends; of blood-red mimosas in Victoria Park, cerulean blue quilted rickshaw covers, yellow soft-as-powder sands of Pei-tai-ho Beach; of the silvery bridge joining the French and Italian concessions; of murky green water of the Hai-Ho Canal; of white signs that said, "No dogs or Chinese allowed"; and of the blackness into which war had plunged us.

As the years progressed and the doors of China seemed locked shut forever, my childhood there seemed more like a dream and not a reality. The colors and people of my dreams became more vivid, richer, more varied, more tormenting, more satisfying, more intense. It was then, by necessity, that the writing began. For me, writing about growing up as a Jewish girl in Tientsin was a way to anchor my misty, dreamy past, a way to bring the universe of my dreams into the present. I felt that if I hewed blocks of memories into a mighty forest of words and scenes, somehow I would create substance out of the transparencies of my dreams. Writing seemed the only way to make myself part of that world once again.

And so memory and emotion, fact and fiction have merged themselves to form this collection of stories.

1. *Beginnings*

Origins

I SPRING FROM two umbilical cords. On my father's side the umbilical cord of my ancestral beginnings is steeped in the loamy terrain of Siberia, in towns with strange names. Vladivostok, Khaborovsk, Tsimmermanovka. On my maternal side it is Ekatrinburg, Komushlov, and Stantsiya Zapodnaya Dvina. I have difficulty locating them on standard maps. They fester in my memory, small internal wounds wanting to be healed. I buy bigger and bigger atlases, tracing the river Amur with my fingers, willing one of them to appear. The day I found Tsimmermanovka on the *New York Times Atlas* map I felt like Columbus sighting land after months at sea, Marie Curie discovering the streaks of radium. Somewhere within them a bolt of recognition must have exploded. In the night quiet of the local library I too made the sightings and exploded with discoverer's joy.

In my dreams both umbilical cords writhe and vibrate with ceaseless energy. I am attached to them and they push me forward. I hang on to them and they pulsate with life's force. Generations of boundless vigor and endurance have been passed on to me from both sides.

With my great-grandfather Abraham Tsimmerman, truth and fiction have produced a filmy, smudged image, handled and rehandled by numerous family members through the years. He was, according to story, a fifteen-year-old, conscripted into the czar's army around 1849. I am told he was "plucked from the streets of Irkutsk to serve in the army and no notice was ever given to him or his parents. The czar ruled all and no questions asked." In the army they tried to convert him from Judaism to Russian Orthodoxy, but he was not won over. Some say he finally ran away from the czar's army and found himself in Siberia—far away from his birthplace in Irkutsk. I think of him alone on the banks of the Amur, listening to the crackling of ice floes, possibly the only Jew within miles, his family far away.

The hamlet of Tsimmermanovka is named after him. He must have done something to earn this privilege, must have risen to some heights in the community. Perhaps they were impressed with the ceaseless energy of this outsider who made good against all odds, creating a successful business and a large family. He died before my father was born, who was, in accordance with Jewish tradition, named after the Amur squatter.

My grandfather, David Tsimmerman, was born in Khaborovsk but soon settled in Vladivostok. In 1916 Czar Nicholas II had five hundred copies of his commemorative book about the Romanoff dynasty circulated in the country. Its pages glorified the past and exalted the present achievements of the empire. Somewhere in the middle of this heavy tome with covers embossed in silver is a half page dedicated to my grandfather. He looks gentle, with dreamy eyes, as he does in the few other pictures I have of him.

Somewhere in him the artistic and the business-mindedness merged to produce what the books describe as an "outstanding citizen." He had by then amassed a fortune, owning a flour mill, a lumberyard that sent lumber to London, a railroad with its own trains and modern equipment, and a meat plant that supplied the local garrison in Vladivostok. His house at 46 Borodinskaya had eight rooms.

Grandfather David was one of six brothers, and the clan was a powerful force in Vladivostok's business world. Among them they owned a silver mine in Tiv Te Khe, the *Hanamet* (a steamship), and several hotels. Their houses dominated the two main boulevards in town—Borodinskaya and Kitaiskaya. There were occasional flurries of anti-Semitism, but these were tolerated and accepted as irritating inconveniences. The expression of Jewish tradition was left to the women and tolerated with a smile.

My father spent his first twenty-five years in Vladivostok in the house on Borodinskaya, where he grew up, the third child of six. "He was always

*My mother's
mother.*

his mother's favorite—she spoiled him," I used to hear about him, as if
thus explaining away his sensitivity, his romanticism, his dreamy piano
playing, his vacillating moods, his ceaseless and often unfocused energy,
and his lack of entrepreneurial skills. He was a good student and a member of the Young Zionist organization that met in the library of his father's home. In most of his early pictures he stands sideways, away from
the glare of the photographer's flash, as if poised for flight from light that
was too harsh to bear.

Facts are sparsely scattered on my maternal side. It is, of course, entirely
possible that stories were told, but I didn't listen, so dazed I was by my
elegant, romantic father. What I do know is that my great-grandmother
sold herring, owned a house in Dvinsk, and built a synagogue in that city.
Grandmother Anya owned a matzo- and rope-making factory in Me-
stechko Kraslavka near Moscow, and the family summered in Stantsiya
Zapodnaya Dvina. In the background, like churning giants, loomed mil-
lionaire relatives making fortunes in furs and bristles. Grandmother Anya,
a bundle of energy and a woman of fierce determination, realizing the lack
of educational opportunities for her children, sent her eldest, my mother,
to Harbin, Manchuria, to one of these wealthy uncles. My mother, who
was twelve at the time, traveled from west to east across the vast prairies

My father's mother (right) with my aunt.

and mountains of Russia for six months. The journey was tedious and frightening, each stop along the way fraught with anxiety as the White and Red armies clashed in a bloody civil war. When she finally reached her destination, it was the summer of 1917. Once a hamlet of mud-brick huts surrounded by fields, Harbin had become the administrative center of the Chinese Eastern Railway, a burgeoning and vital trade center.

In the early twenties my father and his family steamed on their boat, the *Hanamet*, to Tientsin to wait out the Russian Revolution. Thinking that it would only last a while, they brought little with them. From Harbin, my mother and her uncle's family came to Tientsin to expand the family business of furs and bristles. I am told that Tientsin then was a gay, lively, commercially booming city. Many nationalities were finding their place in this Chinese city, which was open and eager for business ventures. Each created its own minicountry in Tientsin, each "concession" with its own

My parents.

laws, bureaucracy, and buildings. Winding through the Italian, French, English, and German concessions was Victoria Road, tree-lined and filled with white-marbled banks and office buildings. Strung along this avenue were the landmarks of Tientsin: Gordon Hall, a stately building housing the English offices; Astor House, the most elegant hotel in town, with a curving staircase; Victoria Park, with two crimson-tiled pagodas and benches with latticed awnings where Chinese amahs tended their charges; Kiessling's, the favored bakery and cafe where on Sundays quartets of musicians ground out Vienna waltzes. Having no concession of our own, we Jews were spread throughout Tientsin. The Jewish Club Kunst was our fulcrum, the center of all the community's doings.

In 1925 my parents met and married in Tientsin. Four years later, I was born in a Catholic hospital on Mercy Road, attended, I am told, by coolly remote nuns who did not respond to my young mother's cries for help

Me in
Victoria Park.

until their prayers were over. Perhaps they were not too eager to receive
yet another Jewish child.

I grew up nourished tenderly by both parents. Because he always
dreamt out loud, my father was my choicest childhood companion. He began to read to me at an early age, treating me to hilarious sessions with the
Russian humorist Zhoschenko and awakening in me the love of words. He
read Chekhov and Tolstoy and Pushkin, and I fell in love with the sheer

grace and cadence of their vocabulary. I developed into a watchful child, as dreamy and imaginative as my father.

During my childhood my father first worked as a broker—buying and selling peanuts, which were then sent on to San Francisco. But the job that most satisfied him was working as an administrative assistant to the Swiss consul, a man he greatly revered and loved and to whom he gave his ceaseless and untiring energy, exalting the man to an almost godlike status. For many years he filled my mind with dreams of moving to Switzerland.

But it was from my mother that I got what is necessary to become an adult. It was she who was in charge of paying bills, planning meals, arranging for piano lessons, taking me to the dentist. She moved in a world outside of my own and my father's peripheries, smoothing the way, making things happen. Without her, life would have been a difficult, tangled affair. With her, it flowed like a tightly wound skein of wool. She excused, perhaps even encouraged, my father and me in our frivolous play, our fanciful flights of imagination. Perhaps she instinctively knew that a child needs both solid ground and fluffy skies. I grew up combining both in my nature. From the ceaseless energy of the dreamy Amur squatter, my paternal great-grandfather, and from the energetic herring-selling entrepreneur, my maternal grandmother, I inherited a pulsating, vibrant vision of life.

My Amah

MY LONG HAIR, worn in braids, is prone to snarly tangles. Every morning Amah stands behind me undoing the knots. Her hands are delicate, tiny birdlike claws that gently but methodically tease out the unruly loops. We do not talk. I dream about cool, chlorinated swimming pools, about slicing into the water like a clean knife, about new red shoes with almost-grown-up heels. My thoughts, soft and lazy, hum behind my eyes. I do not see her, but I know she is there behind me, dressed in faded blue pants and jacket. Her feet are bound, misshapen triangular sheaves. She pads around the house on them, leaving and entering rooms with no sound.

Every person of any means in my town has an amah. Diminutive Chinese women—nannies—peasant women brought to the city to do menial service in *vaigo zhen* (white people's) homes. They leave their own children to tend those of others. Whole villages empty of mothers, their main economy based on their expatriate women. Solemn, black-eyed children living muted, motherless lives.

I've seen my amah dictate letters to a scribe. I've seen her look into the distance as she talks to the scribe, but I don't know what she is saying. I know no Chinese at all.

It's all done, she now says, as she puts down the silver embossed comb and brush set on my cerulean blue vanity. It's all done.

My amah (left) and our rickshaw boy, Tsui (center), with his family.

When the rain comes down in torrential sheets, I leave my shoes outside the door and walk in barefoot. Amah is there the moment I open the door, silent as a waiting sentinel, and brings a chair for me to sit on. She lowers herself like a melting dancer and rubs my feet, blowing her hot breath to warm them. I look down at her shiny black hair, brutally parted in the middle, separating the head into two severe, symmetrical black halves. Her hot breath engulfs me like an incendiary plume. She motions me to take off my wet clothes, which she folds and carries out of the room, drops of rain sliding off them, which she then carefully mops up with her tiny bound foot. She comes back with fresh, neatly ironed clothes.

My amah knows the crooks and crannies of my body, she knows my scent, has intimate knowledge of the stains left on my underwear, knows that the snarls on the left side of my head are more unmanageable, has seen the wrinkles left by my body on an unmade bed. I know nothing about her. Not even her name.

When the heels on my red shoes flatten out from constant wear, I give them to Amah and tell her she can send them to her children. She thanks me demurely, eyes cast down. I imagine them on the feet of a once shoe-less child, perhaps my age; a dusty hamlet now brightened by alien red footwear. How many children does she have? I don't know and don't ask. They are "the children" and she is "Amah."

My father brings Buddy home one day. He is a shivering, matted puppy with two of his legs badly crushed. He was found whimpering under a rickshaw. Soon Buddy's legs heal, but he never regains his ability to control his urinary functions. He leaves shiny little puddles all over the house— pungent, clearly defined dark spots on our glossy parquet floors—and they become another of Amah's chores. She is constantly vigilant and follows him from room to room. He leads her a merry chase, his little furry face gleeful. She mutters words under her breath, but I am not sure what she is saying. They sound like angry sizzled spit.

I have a dream one night that Amah kills Buddy, slowly, methodically, chopping him with the same cleaver she uses to chop vegetables for our dinner. In the dream she complains to a group of faceless Chinese women that the white people's dog has made life miserable for her. They all nod their heads in unison, crescent-moon blank faces. She chops and they nod.

I wake up in a sweat and see a dazzling moon hanging so close to my window that it looks like a holiday lantern. Creeping out of my room, I journey to Amah's. She sleeps only a few feet away from me, in a tiny, windowless servant's room. She lies on a thin mattress, covered with a quilt. I watch her breathe, each breath so slight, faint, almost apologetic. I stand there for a long time, then close the door to her room and go back to bed. I will bury my dream in a deep cavity and cover it with soft quilts.

She did everything for me and I never did a thing for her. I should have, but I didn't know how.

First Day of School

I STAND IN front of the Tientsin American School, holding my mother's hand, knowing only four English words. "May I be excused?" I roll them around in my mouth over and over again. They are my beads of confidence, my amulets, and during that first day in kindergarten I say them many times as the need to excuse myself repeats itself. Each time I am led to a small, shiny bathroom with opalescent tiles, fresh pink towels, and child-size toilets. There is safety in the room and comfort, and I wish I would stay here forever. But a gentle knock on the door reminds me that I need to return.

I am the only non-American child in the classroom in this American Embassy–run school. This insertion into American life was made possible by my Aunt Helen, who is an American citizen and a formidable force in my family. Aunt Helen issues decrees and makes all the important decisions. It was she who decided that the best education for me was in an American school. She told the embassy that she had adopted me, and without requiring any proof of this act (who would have dared oppose her fiery black eyes and chic outfit?), they acknowledged her demands and assigned me to the kindergarten class of Mrs. Fink.

On that first day I fall in love with Mrs. Fink and her classroom, the neat shelves stacked with multicolored books, the wraparound desks so easy to slide into, and the sky-reaching swings in the yard. On Saturday I miss my school with a haunting new ache and sneak into the deserted playground to make sure it and the schoolhouse are still there. Swinging madly and reaching amazing heights, I test my new vocabulary of words, words that even my parents do not know. "My name is Isabelle. I am five years old, and I can speak American," I scream into the wind.

Mimosas Provide Shade

ONE HOT, SHIMMERING day in August, I was barred from entering the convent of Saint Mary Magdalene. I would have welcomed the cool, tiled corridors and the dim interior. The convent was on the outskirts of the European part of Tientsin, settled decades before by nuns whose aim it was to educate and convert the Chinese. When I was eight, I arrived weekly for my French lessons, sitting on the crossbar of my father's bicycle and hearing his labored breathing behind me as he pushed uphill on Davenport Road toward the convent. We rode past the international swimming pool, where later in the day, after the lessons, I would submerge myself in the deliciously cool but highly chlorinated water, past the Min-Yuan soccer grounds now deserted, and past the red-tiled pagodas in Victoria Park. During the summer *fu-tiens* (fierce heat) my father protected himself from the blazing sun by wearing a handkerchief on his head. He tied the four corners into knots, making it look like a little stocking cap. I never wore a hat. You'll never get sunstroke, my mother said. You were born here, so you're a native and immune.

To the north the convent looked out on Davenport Road in the English concession. Its southern gates spilled into rue St. Louis in the French concession. Thus it straddled two worlds with its massive gray structure. The streets were empty this August day, except for some Chinese servants squatting on their haunches in doorways or under dusty mimosa trees, fanning themselves with wide bamboo fans. They sipped hot tea from porcelain cups, the steam from their cups mingling with the afternoon haze.

My father dropped me off at the gate of the convent and said he would be back in an hour to pick me up. I watched his bicycle disappear in the glimmering haze and then walked into the small front garden. As I stood at the carved black door, I felt my red seersucker dress clinging in wet spots to my thighs and midriff, and I ached for the coolness inside.

The door was opened by an unfamiliar nun, who towered over me. She held the door barely ajar with one hand and looked down at me.

"Yes," she said. It was not an affirmative yes or a question; it was almost sung. "Y . . e . . . ss."

"It's Tuesday," I said. "I'm here for my French lesson."

"Ah."

I looked up at her. The folds of her long black habit were shiny in spots. Across her forehead the white bandeau was starched and spotless. There was not a spot of sweat on her face. Mine was damp, and down my back I could feel a trickle of perspiration.

"It's four o'clock. I usually come at four."

"Ye . . . ess," she said again in that undecipherable tone. She looked so cool and remote, so distant. I could not understand why she was not letting me in. I could feel the sun beating on my back.

It occurred to me that perhaps I was early, and looking at my newly acquired wristwatch, I realized it was indeed ten minutes to four.

"I'm ten minutes early. Can I come in to wait for Sister Mathilde?"

She stared at me silently. I noticed that her eyes were bright blue, almost purple. "Turn around," she said in a soft but commanding voice.

"Turn around?"

"Yes."

I turned around, slowly pivoting on my feet, and realized with embarrassment that she would see the streaks of sweat on my back. I wondered how many layers of clothing she wore underneath her habit and how she managed to keep cool.

After examining me for what seemed a full five minutes, she said, "You can't come in today."

"Can't come in! Why not?"

"Your dress has no back. And no sleeves."

"But I always wear this kind of dress in the summer. They're halter dresses, you know. To keep cool in the summer."

"You cannot come into the house of the Lord dressed this way. It's disrespectful."

"Sister Mathilde let me in last week. And the week before."

She was silent for a while, and then for the first time she looked away from me. "Sister Mathilde is a novice."

"But where will I wait? My father won't pick me up for another hour." I panicked at the thought of sitting in the sun without any shade for a whole hour.

"Find something to do. Go over your lessons."

I looked at her helplessly. She still had her hand on the door. There seemed nothing more inviting at this moment than the thought of cool checkered tiles under my blistering feet.

"Qui est là?" (Who is there?) I heard a voice from the interior.

"C'est la petite Juive pour ca leçon" (It is the little Jewish girl who's come for her lesson), said the nun. She started closing the door.

"But there is no shade outside," I said.

"Yes." Again that enigmatic tone. "We *will* be planting mimosa next year." She turned around and started to walk away. I took a step forward, about to ask her what she meant, but she closed the door and I found myself alone on the steps.

I looked around the unfamiliar garden, realizing I had never spent any time here before. There were no trees—just a few dusty shrubs with gray leaves. A clump of enormous sunflowers in a corner provided a spot of color but no shade. I sat on the steps and fashioned a visor (to protect myself from the sun) out of a piece of paper from my notebook and clipped it onto my hair with two hairpins. I tried reviewing my homework but found myself losing interest. "La petite Juive, la petite Juive," ran the words in my head over and over again. The disembodied voice from the convent's interior had not been a harsh one, but the words made me shiver even as the sun beat down on me. Listlessly I wandered around the cramped garden, kicking small round stones in the dust and hoping my father would come soon, but given his punctuality I knew he would arrive exactly on the hour.

A giant spider, exposed by one overturned stone, scuttled to safety, its body quivering under a layer of dust. A Chinese servant came out from the convent and began to sweep the stairs but soon gave up this endeavor, as the puffs of dust hung briefly in the thick air and then settled back on the steps.

At exactly five o'clock my father waved to me through the garden gate without getting off his bicycle, and I ran to meet him. I climbed on the crossbar and we rode silently, as we often did, through the quiet streets, the sun still beating relentlessly on our backs. When we got home my mother inquired how the lesson was. "I never had a lesson." I told her I hadn't been allowed inside the convent because of my halter dress. "My new red seersucker dress," I pointed out, "the pretty one."

My mother was puzzled. "Didn't you go in that dress last week?"

"Yes," I said, "but today she wouldn't let me in, the tall nun. She said Sister Mathilde had let me in because she is a novice. What's a novice?"

"A novice is someone new and inexperienced. Sister Mathilde probably is new at the convent and doesn't know the rules." My mother sat tapping her forehead with her fingers, as she often did when making a decision. "We'll just have to think of something to get around this problem. I'll come up with something," she said cheerily.

Just before dinner my mother said she had come up with a marvelous idea. She told me we would sew little capes for my halter dresses, which I would wear on the days of my lessons, thus covering my back and arms. I looked at her to see if she was joking, but there was not even a quiver of a smile on her face.

"Why do I have to do that?"

"Because it's their house and their rules. You have to be proper when you go there and not offend anyone. Besides, it's the best place to learn French. You know that, so don't put up a fuss."

"Why?" I persisted.

"You have to learn to accommodate, to put up with certain things. You'll understand when you're older."

My mother went on to tell me how tomorrow we would go to see Mrs. Feldman, who had sewn the original backless dresses, and order some "little cute capes" for them.

"I hate capes," I said. "Fania Stoffman wears them and she's a hunchback." I often saw Fania in the streets, her head bent low, scuttling close to the walls as if trying to blend in, wearing ugly orthopedic shoes and caped dresses to cover her hump.

"Hush," my mother said, and the subject was closed.

Next day my mother and I went to see Mrs. Feldman. We went in the evening when it was cooler. Mrs. Feldman lived in an alley, and her two small rooms were littered with bolts of fabric, old *Vogue* magazines, and Montgomery Ward catalogs from the United States. A sister in Pasadena sent them regularly to her before the war, and it was out of these magazines, some months back, that I had chosen the halter dresses for summer. Darting around the room, Mrs. Feldman showed us various kinds of cloth and suggested a cape of contrasting material. She said she could have the cape fasten with little hooks, so it could easily come off. Draping several pieces of cloth around her shoulder, and with her mouth full of pins, Mrs. Feldman danced around me, explaining to my mother how it would all work. "We'll start a new trend, a new fashion," she sang.

I felt gloomy and tired when we left Mrs. Feldman. "I'm going to look just like Fania. A hunchback," I kept muttering to my mother. "I could just wear my other dresses—the ones with sleeves."

"They're too hot for summer wear. This way, you wear the cape only on Tuesdays, for one hour. Once you leave the convent, you can whip it off and you'll be in your fashionable halter dress."

"But why can't you talk to the nuns and ask them to let me wear what I want?"

My mother stopped suddenly in the middle of the street and released my hand, which she had been holding. There was a puzzled look on her face, and she squeezed her eyebrows as if in pain. "I can't talk to the nuns," she said. "I even pay them by mail."

"But why? Why can't you talk to them?"

"They're Catholic. It's a different world. They live in their world, and we in ours. Someday you'll understand. Come on; how about an ice cream cone at Kiessling's Cafe?"

I did not understand at all. Things seemed to be getting more and more bewildering all the time. "La petite Juive, la petite Juive." The phrase kept repeating itself in my head, as if the needle was stuck in the groove.

We walked silently the two blocks to Kiessling's, where I had my favorite ice cream. I ordered Kiessling's special, called the *kuchka*—a cool mound of chocolate and wafers—but somehow it didn't taste as delicious as usual. I must have been sitting glumly, because my mother suggested we go see a movie, an activity usually reserved only for Saturday afternoons. I declined, saying I was tired and wanted to go home.

My mother brought home two little capes during the next week. Both she and my father oohed and aahed over them, saying what a genius Mrs. Feldman was. They were reversible, so actually I had four capes, and they flowed from my shoulders like wings. "I'm sure the nuns will approve," they both exclaimed.

My father deposited me on the doorsteps of Saint Mary Magdalene the next week at the usual time. Just before we got to the gate, he got off the bicycle and helped me fasten the cape to my dress. "It's really quite attractive," he said.

I looked at my tall, handsome father, leaning against the bicycle. "Why?" I said. "Why can't I wear what I want?"

My father sighed, patted me on the head, and said, "Cheer up." Then he started laughing, leaned toward me, and whispered into my ear. "The cape makes you look like an angel. They look like wings sprouting from your back. Now you'll really fit in, the little Jewish angel." I thought of the fat little angels in the pictures and sculptures in the convent and began to laugh. We both roared.

"There now, feel better?" he said.

"Yes," I said, even though the cape was scratching my wet skin. I walked toward the convent door, and it was Sister Mathilde who answered it. I hesitated, wondering if she would ask me to turn around.

"Come in, come on in," she said and waved me inside.

I walked behind her, down the long, dim corridor with the cool tiled floor, past the white alabaster statues gleaming in the dark. At the end of the corridor I could see the anguished statue of Christ, and as usual I averted my eyes when we came close to the half-naked figure, wondering how come it was all right for him to be naked while I had to be fully dressed, cape and all. Sister Mathilde bent one knee in front of the statue, her black dress spreading like a fan behind her. I waited while she performed her ceremony, feeling slightly nauseous and glad when she was through and we could go upstairs, along another dim hallway to the classroom. There we sat at our usual place by the window, and Sister Mathilde told me to start reading the second chapter of *Les Misérables*.

A fly was buzzing in the corner of the room as I read out loud. The afternoon heat parched my throat, and I asked Sister Mathilde if I could get a drink of water. As I got up, I gently swayed the wings of my "nifty" cape, hoping that she would notice and give me a sign of approval. I glanced back at her as I was leaving the room. She was looking out the window, her head tilted slightly to the right, her alabaster-white finger stroking her lip. Without turning her head, she muttered dreamily, "The *fu-tiens* will soon be over. And we *will* be planting mimosa. In a few years they will provide shade for us." I stopped in the doorway, wondering if she would say more. She must know about last week's incident, I thought to myself. But Sister Mathilde continued to look out the window and was quiet. My head was aching from the heat, and I welcomed the cool water from the fountain as it slithered down my parched throat.

Land of Outcasts

I STUFF CHUNKS of cotton wool in my ears in the middle of the night so as not to hear the muffled shouts and cries coming from the next room. Scary questions, like fiery plumes, singe my brain. "Why do you always fight?" I want to say to my parents, but the question dies stillborn. In the morning I search for telltale signs—some disarray, reddened eyes, a tiredness. But my parents are always bright, cheery, and dewy with life. They love me and deceive me with a full heart.

Sometimes I take out the cotton wool, and then I hear them.

"Stuck in China, this godforsaken land," my father's voice thunders.

"But life is good here. Easy and good," my mother chirps.

"This is the land of outcasts, country of stateless refugees," he roars.

"Hush, you'll wake her," she whispers.

"We must get out of here . . . somehow," he growls harshly.

The ping-pong of their debate rattles the windows and reverberates like an earthquake in the soles of my feet. Last night they yelled, hurling words like "marriage" and "loyalty" in thunderous bouquets. Each night a different theme explodes. I snuggle deeper into the moist, steamy world beneath my peacock quilt, armed with wads of cotton wool so that I can, at will, block the world from entering, comforting myself with their sunny daytime love and despising the black currents of their night. I have no debate. I want to stay here forever. This is my land.

Braverman, DP

BRAVERMAN WAS A DP. Displaced person. He came into my life cautiously and departed several months later, almost without a perceptible trace. What he left was a smudge on my membranes, one that I could never rub out, that became as familiar as the smallpox stamp on my left thigh. I was ten when he slipped into my life, and he, I thought, was ancient. For three months a thin wall separated my room from his.

At the time, we lived at my grandmother's house on Davenport Road across the street from the thickly walled British Embassy and several blocks from the sluggishly yellow Hai-ho Canal. My grandmother lived in the front room downstairs, the one closest to the door, so she could be the first to answer a ringing doorbell. Her room was filled with lavishly framed photographs of relatives around the world. Cousin Ethel, who looked like Loretta Young, from San Francisco, Aunt Haya from Australia, and Aunt Dina from New York. I had never been outside North China. Often I stood before them, trying to penetrate the world beyond the stiff photographic poses, but all I saw was the stock studio backdrops.

My parents and I had two rooms upstairs. Across the hall from us lived my aunt and uncle. The fourth upstairs room was occupied by Mrs. Leff, an elderly widow. Downstairs was the Brachtman family—mother, father, and son. Mrs. Kipness and her daughter, Vera, shared the room next to Grandmother. The room closest to the kitchen was settled by the Lerman family—mother, father, son Ben, and grand piano. In a wing off the kitchen, in two dingy and windowless rooms, lived our two Chinese servants. Although they had been with my grandmother for years, they were known simply as Cook and Boy.

A total of seventeen souls ate, slept, conversed, made love, quarreled and made up, cried and laughed under my grandmother's roof. All activity was muted and hushed, performed discreetly and with an exquisite awareness of the proximity of others.

One bathroom served the entire household, and everyone got a turn without a push or a shove. Bodily functions were bravely accommodated, and an unwritten schedule was strictly adhered to. Folks downstairs had first turn, folks upstairs went second. Mrs. Leff was given special preference because of her age and was pushed forward to first place whenever she arrived. "Thank you, thank you," she would whisper shyly. Mrs. Kipness, although not elderly, also got preferential treatment because of her "delicate stomach." With eyes demurely cast down, she too would slide to the front of the line. Children went last.

One day as we stood in line, my mother, holding the towel and bar of soap for both of us, said, "You are going to have to give up your playroom."

"Why? It's not really a room, anyway. It's just a closet." I was referring to the large unused closet with a window that separated my room from my parents'. Doorless, and too small to be used as a living space, it had been given to me to store dolls and toys. I had grown to love it. My mother had hung a lace curtain on the empty door frame, anchoring it with thumbtacks. Often I lay on the floor watching the sun catch the lacy patterns and then bounce them on the walls. Every day at four in the afternoon I could hear the muted sounds of Ben Lerman's piano practice seep through the floor cracks.

"We're expecting a Mr. Braverman. Rudolf Braverman. A DP. From Germany. He is to have that room."

"When?"

"Tomorrow. You'd better take your things out. Later today." German refugees were trickling into my part of the world. There was a new girl, Eva, in my class, from Berlin. A dentist from Bremen had set up shop on Victoria Road. I had visited a new ear, nose, and throat specialist from Hamburg who had opened up a practice on Mercy Road.

"It's only a closet. Not big enough for a person. And it's right next to my room, just inches away from my bed," I wailed, panicking at the invasion of a strange man. "Will a door be put up?" I pleaded. "Maybe, if we have time," my mother replied. I imagined the man, no doubt with a hideous guttural accent, probably speaking only German, a stranger, an alien, plunked down in my midst. New people coming into the community was one thing, but a total stranger right in my own house, next door to me, was totally unacceptable.

"Well, the place is big enough for a single man. It will have to do. He can't pay much rent." My mother disappeared into the bathroom for her turn.

"What's a DP?" I asked Ben, who was standing behind me in line. Ben, who had a head that looked far too big for his body, wore oversized horn-rimmed glasses and was often described by people as a "genius, he'll go far someday." He bared his lips as if he were about to spit and said, "A displaced person, you dummy. Don't you know? Braverman has escaped from the Nazis. Probably has been tortured, probably is very sick, probably has lost oodles of family. I hear his daughter was murdered. They never tell us anything, but I hear. I listen."

I didn't like Ben, but I respected him. He seemed to understand the adult world, living on the peripheries of their talk and gossip, often allowed to stay behind during conversations when I was told to "go and play." His story about the coming of Braverman did not reassure me. Now I would have not only a stranger in my midst but possibly a sick stranger with a murdered child. Maybe she had been my age. What was her name? I wondered. A taut sliver of excitement coursed through me, and I leaned against the wall for support.

Later that day I transported my belongings back to my room. My mother took down the lace curtain and in its place hung a thick, faded quilt. Cook and Boy brought up a camp bed and a small night table. Nails were pounded into the walls. A tall, spindly lamp with a faded fringed lamp shade that didn't fit and had to be tied with a string completed the decor. "Well, it's ready for Mr. Braverman," my mother told me. "He's been through a lot, he'll be tired."

All day I peered out of my window, stood at the front door, even went outside in the garden to watch for Braverman. I wanted to see him before he saw me. I wanted to know the size, shape, and smell of the intruder. It would be like seeing the operating room before I had my tonsils out. Seeing him first would give me an advantage, an upper hand. I lay in wait for Braverman, but he never showed up.

I went to bed in a room overflowing with toys from the playroom. In the middle of the night I woke up, as I often did, listening to the night sounds. I heard Mrs. Leff's furtive coughs, the rattling of the spoon against glass as she mixed cough medication with hot water from the kettle on the burner she kept in her room. The steps creaked as someone from downstairs crept upstairs to the bathroom. A few minutes later the muffled flush of the toilet. The tapping of the broken shutter against the outside wall. Familiar sounds. Now a new sound was added, one that I could not describe. A tiny crackling sound, soft and rustling. It was coming from the closet! *Crack. Whirr.* What was it? I tried, but could not define it. Sleep overcame me as the surrounding quiet of the house embraced me. I dreamt of giant mice munching on strange red pellets while in the background Ben played the "Moonlight Sonata" with relentless vigor, over and over again.

Next morning, toothbrush and towel in hand, I met a stranger in the hall. He too carried a toothbrush and towel, both of us obviously heading for the bathroom. I was surprised to find him so small and thin-boned. Wispy white hair hung around his ears, a scraggly moustache hid his lips. He walked airily on the balls of his feet as if contact with the ground was painful. Seeing me, he hesitated, looked around furtively, and lowered his hooded eyes. He whispered something in a foreign language—it sounded like an apology—clicked his heels, and retreated, crablike, into the closet. He reminded me of the sea anemones I used to disturb at the beach, which would close up and back away from my invasive toe. The thought that I could be the invader was an intriguing one. And he a frightened grown-up?

Brushing my teeth at top speed, I combed my hair and rushed back to my room. Leaning into the quilt as much as I could without disturbing its folds, I tried to hear what was going on inside the closet. I knew Braverman must be in there, I had seen him go in, but there were no sounds, no movements coming from the other side of the quilt. I curbed the urge to move the quilt, to peek in, feeling that that would constitute a raid. Somewhere in me burgeoned the ideas of fairness, of privacy, of delicacy. I was learning patience.

For the next few days I did not see Braverman at all. He was obviously avoiding me and had established a bathroom routine that did not coincide with mine. I imagined him creeping out of his closet when most of the household had gone to work, or maybe waiting till midnight when we were asleep. The fact that Braverman was making all these plans to dodge me filled me with a sense of wonderment. I ached to boast about it to Ben but decided against it. Ben, no doubt, would put me down or offer a totally different explanation filled with words I could not understand.

Several nights later I was again awakened by the crackling sounds. This time I forced myself to stay awake and listen intently. They were definitely coming from the closet. There was no light there. Whatever Braverman was doing, he was doing it in total darkness. I heard the creak of his camp bed, the scraping of something heavy against the floor. I heard the popping sound of a paper bag being opened. Followed by evenly spaced crackling sounds. I ran down the list of possible things that could make such a noise: He was sorting things in his suitcase. Brushing his teeth. Scratching the wall. Burying small bodies—this option gave me goose bumps. Finally I decided that Braverman was shelling peanuts in the middle of the night. The sounds went on for at least half an hour, and then I heard the paper bag being shut. I felt a surge of victory at my first discovery. Braverman was a night eater and he ate peanuts.

Just as I was about to doze off, I saw a shadow in my doorway. (I always left my door ajar because of night terrors.) A small bundle of fear settled in my ribs as I watched this ghostly apparition. It did not move, just kept looking in my direction. Then he started crooning a song, the words of which I could not understand, but they were strangely soothing and vaguely familiar. I fell asleep.

Early next morning, on my way to the bathroom, I met Braverman in the hall. It was earlier than my usual time, and I expect that he had not anticipated seeing me. He was fully dressed in a shabby suit, shiny at the elbows and wrists. A crumpled fedora with grease spots and well-worn shoes with patches on the sides completed the outfit. He was carrying a battered briefcase with a broken clasp. I must have startled him, for he stood frozen in his tracks, gasping short bursts of air as if to make himself even smaller than he actually was. I had the feeling that he wanted to disappear, to evaporate in front of me. He held the briefcase close to his body as if burying himself in it.

I smiled at Braverman, and a bevy of questions erupted in my mind. Why do you eat peanuts in the middle of the night? Why do you eat in the dark? Do you need a better lamp? A flashlight? Was that you standing in my doorway? What was the song you sang? But all I said was "Good morning." He stared at me, then in a raspy voice that sounded like it came from a deep well, whispered, "Guten Morgen" and scurried away. There was a strange look in his eyes, a look of terror and yearning. It was a look I had never seen before, but I was strangely unfrightened by it.

On my way out I met Ben—both of us going to school. We never walked together but occasionally exchanged a few words on the front steps. I had absolutely no desire to be seen with Ben. "The weird one," my friends called him.

"What's it like sleeping right next to Braverman?" he said.

"I'm not sleeping next to Braverman," I indignantly replied. "Braverman has his room and I have mine."

"He's a queer duck," whispered Ben.

"What do you mean—queer?"

"Never talks to anyone. I started a conversation with him, asked him about Hitler. He just looked past me and fled."

"Maybe he doesn't want to talk about some things," I said, proud of my observations.

Ben glared at me. "It's his history. Makes him strange. Wanna hear something? Well, yesterday I heard Mrs. Kipness tell Mrs. Leff that Braverman spent several years in hiding. In a dark cellar. With rats. All over him. Mrs. Kipness said it was totally dark in the cellar, and they had to lower his food to him through a hole in the floor."

"You're making it up."

"I am not," said Ben and started walking away.

"All right, come back. Tell me more."

"Well," said Ben coming back to me with a smirk on his face. "Well, Mrs. Leff then said she had heard that the rest of his entire family—

wife, daughter, and mother—were taken away one night when he was gone. He came back to the apartment, and there was no one there, and he went off."

"What do you mean 'off'?" I said with irritation. Ben had a way with implications, looks, indications that drove me crazy.

"Off. Cuckoo. Crazy. Mrs. Leff says he went on a rampage and killed someone. That very night."

"You're making it all up," I gasped. "You're making up stories."

Ben was unshaken. "And you know what else I think? I think Braverman may have killed other people with poison."

"Why poison?" I shrieked.

"Because I heard Mrs. Kipness say that Braverman used to be a pharmacist and you know . . ." Ben's voice trailed off.

"You know . . . what?" I screamed.

"Well, they have access to all sorts of drugs and poisons." Ben looked at his Mickey Mouse watch. "Time to go." I watched him hoist his book satchel over his shoulder and lope off.

Part of me was convinced that Ben was making up stories about Braverman, that he was showing off, making up for his lack of friends by weaving tales. But he did hang around grown-ups and was able to pick up bits and pieces of forbidden information. I shivered feverishly, thinking of Braverman as a murderer. There was gentleness, there was sadness, mystery, but there was absolutely nothing abrasive or violent about Braverman. Ben must be wrong. But there was something to the story that rang true—the fact that Braverman used to eat at night in the cellar without light. He was used to eating in darkness.

For weeks I tried to time my bathroom routine with the comings and goings of Braverman, but he continued to evade me. At times I still woke up to the shelling of peanuts. Once I dreamt that he was standing beside my bed and softly crying. He carried an object in his arms that I suspected was a gun or an axe, and I woke up in a sweat to see him standing in the doorway, staring into space. Silhouetted against the moon, his cheeks glistened as if with tears.

"It's a nice night," I whispered into the dark, feeling a great urge to comfort him.

Braverman shuddered, reeled as if hit by a sharp object, and scuttled back into the closet without a word. I felt a strange protectiveness for him, the kind of feeling I used to have for wounded animals. Once I had tamed a frightened, quivering little squirrel by sitting very quietly at a distance. It had taken weeks for the timid creature to take something from my hand. I would wait for Braverman.

I went about the business of growing up as summer drew near and the mimosas bloomed blood-red. I went to piano lessons with Mrs. Hohlach-kin and dance class at Mme. Voitenko's School of Dance. I waited for summer to begin and education to stop. Braverman and I had reached a comfortable plateau. We never spoke, but I let him stand in my doorway and look at me. He never came inside the room, as if there were a magi-cal line that separated his world from mine, a line not to be crossed. From my bed I listened to his night eating.

Early one morning I lay in bed, feeling the onset of a cold and with it the delicious thought of not going to school, and through slitty-crusty eyes watched the door being pushed forward slowly. A hand appeared and gently deposited a bag precisely in the doorway. I listened for disappearing foot-steps, but there were none. My cold-fogged brain dreamt it was Braverman and that he had flown away, like a bird, into the morning sun. Groggily I got up to pick up the bag, which was tied with a red string. Inside were two dozen peanuts. They were all shiny and plump, not a wizened one among them. Obviously care had been taken with this gift, and a certain cockiness brewed gently in me as I contemplated the attention bestowed on me.

Later that afternoon we met in the hallway. I, in my rumpled housecoat, was on my way to get some hot tea to soothe a gravelly throat. He doffed his hat to me, and with his head still at a rakish angle, looked at me seri-ously from beneath his bushy eyebrows. A dappled sun surrounded us as if we stood in a magic circle, making me feel quite elegant despite my tousled attire. I felt almost grown up. Braverman was probably not ancient at all, I thought. Maybe middle-aged.

Coming home from school one day, I saw Braverman sitting by himself at a table in Victoria Cafe. He was wolfing down a bowl of soup, his hat still on, his small body perched on the edge of the chair as if prepared for flight. I noticed the bobbing of his Adam's apple with every swallow and his twitching left leg. It was the first time I had ever seen him outside our house and the first time I had ever seen him eat. He looked smaller, furtive, secretive. Suddenly he looked up and caught me staring. He began to tremble, got up shakily, leaving a pile of uneaten food on his plate, and looked around as if he had been caught in an obscene act. "Mr. Braverman," I said, "I didn't mean to disturb you. Go on eating." But the glass that separated us was too thick and he did not hear me. He disappeared into the bowels of the restaurant, moving toward the kitchen, avoiding the front door. I toyed with the idea of running to the back door and confronting him but decided against it. Confronting wounded animals was not the best way to get their attention.

The next day I ran into Braverman outside Vassili's Deli on Dickenson Road. What stunned me was that this time he was actually talking to someone. A woman with lots of lipstick, a tight red skirt, very tall heels, and a high pompadour hairstyle. He didn't see me until I got quite close to him. Then he looked around wildly, a frozen grin on his face. Perspiration ran down his cheeks, and he wiped at it with a huge flowered handkerchief. Hurriedly, he left his companion and careened down the street, bumping into people, loping along in a zigzag manner, coattail flying. I watched until he disappeared around the corner, wondering what I had done to cause this crazed flight. His companion, seeming quite nonchalant about the whole episode, lit a cigarette and vanished into the deli. Perhaps she was a Nazi sent to kill him. Or question him. Maybe she had brought bad news. Or maybe she had brought good news from Germany and he was so excited he just danced away.

I decided to approach Ben, even though I knew he might laugh at me.

"You ninny," whinnied Ben, predictably sarcastic. "You're a total ninny. Braverman was making contact with a prostitute. He saw you, got embarrassed, and fled. That's all there is to it. A Nazi agent indeed. You're crazy."

"What's a prostitute?" I questioned humbly.

"Grow up! Don't you know? All right. A prostitute is a woman who engages in promiscuous sexual intercourse for money."

"How do you know that?" I squeaked, overwhelmed by the long series of unfamiliar words all in one sentence, torn between making a fool of myself and inciting Ben's wrath.

"Because I read the dictionary. Don't you ever read the dictionary?" Ben asked, staring at me with his watery eyes, half hidden behind his glasses.

"No. But why was he embarrassed? Why did he run away?"

Ben threw up his hands. "Because you are a child. Because I guess he likes you—heaven knows why. Because he doesn't want you to know he does those things. Maybe because he doesn't want you to tell your grandmother. I don't know. Think for yourself." Ben turned on his heel and left.

I decided to take matters into my own hands. Perhaps Braverman did really like me. Maybe I reminded him of his murdered daughter. Maybe that was why he stood watching me at night. As soon as I could, I would go inside his room and look around. Find clues there and unveil the mystery.

The next day I watched Braverman leave the house with his battered briefcase. With a rapidly beating heart I stood by the quilt, inching toward the part in the middle that would lead me into the privacy of Braverman's nest. I had never seen the place without my array of dolls and toys. What would I find there? Bones? Skeletons of his family? I pulled the quilt aside and quickly stepped in. It was tinier than I had remembered, a small sliver of a room, not more than seven by four feet. The camp bed was meticulously covered with Grandmother's blanket. A faded sweater and a raincoat hung primly, side by side, on two of the nails that had been hammered in. The other two nails stuck out garmentless. There was something pathetic about that. Braverman obviously had only two pieces of clothing. No pictures on the wall, no books, no slippers, no rug, not even a pillow. Instead of a pillow he had neatly rolled up a shirt. There was monumental desolation in the room. I could hear it and smell it.

It felt like the time my favorite dog had died, the time my best friend told me she was moving away, the time when trees are dead in winter and you cannot imagine them ever becoming green again. There were no clues. Only sadness.

"You really shouldn't be here." My mother stood in the doorway.

"It's so . . . sad . . ."

"Mr. Braverman is a sad man. A very sad man."

"Why doesn't he have things? They might make him happier."

"Things probably remind him of the past, the sad past. Things bring back memories and pain. Maybe Mr. Braverman thought if he didn't have things he wouldn't have the pain."

This was an incomprehensible thought. Things had always comforted me. I slept surrounded by my stuffed animals, my two cats at my feet. How could Braverman exist without things? No point in approaching Ben. He had become increasingly irritable lately, and his piano sessions were now three hours long. The rumor in the house was that Ben was studying to go to a conservatory and become a great pianist. Since no one had left town for years, ever since the war had started, it was difficult to imagine what conservatory Ben would go to. I realized then that grown-ups were dreamers and made up things to while away the hours.

I began to dream of giving things to Braverman, to make up for all the things he did not have. Giant red-velvet pillows, thick-piled rugs, a lace tablecloth. But mainly I dreamt of feeding him nectar-sweet pineapples, juicy oranges, and chocolate-covered cherries. With money collected through the years from birthdays, I bought almond and cherry-covered chocolates and my favorite marzipan chocolate wafers. I left them precisely in the middle of his doorway, slipping discreetly back into my room, where I could hear, but not see, his hand pick up the package. There was something delicious in having this arrangement by which things appeared and disappeared silently in doorways.

He continued to leave me bags of peanuts. On the occasions when we met in the hall he now smiled shyly at me, the smile starting tentatively on his upper lip and then growing to the sides of his mouth and even entering his eyes. It was the best Braverman could do, and I loved it.

On June 4 I saw Braverman slinking down the hallway with his brief-case and another small package. He walked downstairs, and then I heard him talking to my grandmother. I bent over the banister to listen.

"I'll never forget your kindness. Never," I heard Braverman's raspy voice saying in Yiddish and some Russian.

"You will be well," I heard my grandmother reply but could not figure out from her intonation whether it was a question or an order.

"I will be well. The job in the cloakroom of Club Kunst will be good. There is a small room—behind the cloakroom—for me."

"If you need help, you know where to come."

"Thank you," replied Braverman, doffing his hat and for some reason lifting his head in my direction. Then he smiled and slightly bowed his head. I heard the door softly closing as he let himself out.

I rushed back to the closet. Maybe he had left something for me. The quilt was gone. When had it been taken down? The place was empty—no cot, no lamp, no night table. Even the nails had been pried from the wall and lay in a small, neat pile on the windowsill. I was about to walk out when I noticed a small bag of peanuts neatly tied with a red string made into a little bow. I opened the package and started eating them.

I sat on the floor, watching the sun's rays, listening to Ben's piano playing, feeling unfathomably happy at having known a sad man, at having seen him smile, at having been watched by him, at having not unfolded the whole mystery, at having the foreign invader turn into an unerasable bump in my heart. We had become accomplices in close living, Braverman and I.

The Pig and I

I AM ON the steps of Anya's house to attend her Russian Orthodox Easter celebrations. I go there every year because we are best friends and because she insists that I come.

In my household there is no discussion of either her Orthodoxy or our Jewishness. Her love for me is fierce, tangled as wild bulrushes. Her slate-blue eyes are pinned tightly to her forehead and so ravishingly savage that they startle me. Our friendship has always felt several sizes too big. Not knowing how to turn down her silky invitations, I come every year.

Slowly I walk to the dining room, where I face the perennial pig. It lies on its sacrificial platter in the middle of an overladen table and dominates the celebrations. Except for the frilly paper collar around its neck and the red shiny crab apple stuck in its dead mouth, it is glisteningly naked. The sightless sockets follow me, and I can feel the hollow eyes on my back even when I am not facing it.

Anya is all smiles and dressed in a torrid black dress far too grown-up for her and which I know she hammered her mother into buying. She offers me *paskha*, which is a mound of heavily pressed cottage cheese studded with raisins and brandied fruits and shaped into a pyramid. She cuts a piece of grainy Easter bread covered with a sugared skirt and topped by a weighty cross speared into its doughy flesh and puts it all on my plate. She regally orders the cook to bring clean plates.

She does not offer me pig; she knows I won't eat it and that we never have pig at home. But she slices it in front of me, her slate-blue eyes intent on the process. I watch the juices squirting in a shower of droplets as the skin is peeled off, slices of its fatty carcass cut, its shoulder prodded with a pointy fork. She thrusts a small piece into her mouth, testing it for succulence, and glances at me behind sooty lashes.

The pig lies meekly, unresisting, its hollow eyes beringed with tear droplets. Anya takes out the crab apple and its mouth now is agape, fixed in a hideous grin, forever silenced. Shivery fingers clutch my spine, and words rumble in my belly but never surface. Like the pig I am mute, shackled in place. I want to run away, hide in the hallway, flee to another world, but nothing moves and Anya is staring me down with her blazing eyes. I stay.

Anya is having a good time; her eyes are moist and her pale yellow bangs are pasted limply on her overheated forehead. I am steeling myself for what is to come. Vodka will flow, food will drip down slack open mouths, jokes will start. First regular jokes, then ethnic jokes. Then, when the grown-ups are totally drunk, Jewish jokes will pop out. "Once there was a Catholic, a Jew . . ." it will start. That's how it was last year and the year before and no doubt next year. It will happen today. I will take a deep breath, eat my food, and plow through the evening. The pig and I, comrades in disaster, will face another year.

Quarantine

IT WAS DURING the matinee showing of *Bambi* at the Empire Theater in Tientsin that I first began to feel sick. As I watched Bambi, her nostrils delicately quivering, fleeing through an eerie fluorescent forest, I felt a tickling at the back of my throat and a throbbing in my left temple. I had stumbled into the dark theater and was now surprised to find myself sitting next to Sima Altman, who was a classmate of mine in the fifth form. "I think I'm getting sick," I whispered to her. "Tell me later; I want to watch the movie," she hissed through clenched teeth and stared straight ahead to the pulsating screen. Sinking into the scratchy mohair seat, I tried to make myself comfortable and squeezed my eyes shut. But the sharp screen lights penetrated my lids and *rat-tat-tat*ted on my eyeballs. I opened one eye and saw Bambi running through a jungle filled with palm fronds that looked like giant hands about to seize her. "What's happening?" I whispered hoarsely to Sima. She silenced me with a poke of her elbow. I sank further into my chair, my head feeling as if giant marbles were crushing each other in my skull.

In the darkness of the theater I felt sorry for myself, having waited three months for the Bambi movie to reach Tientsin. Bambi's face had haunted me for a long time in the posters and advertisements around town. "Be sure your children see the adventures of the shy little fawn," and "A picture not to be missed." Through my hopscotch skills I had won a pack of Bambi playing cards and was the envy of all my friends. Now the day had finally come, and I couldn't even keep my eyes open. I glanced at Sima, who sat immobile, her eyes glued to the screen. Only her hand moved, reaching methodically into a bag of salted sunflower seeds. She brought them delicately to her open mouth. Her teeth glistened in the dark, and her tightly wound braids bobbed up and down on her chest.

I dozed through most of the movie. As the lights went on, I felt an immense heaviness settling in my bones. My legs felt as if lead had been poured into the marrow. "You are slow," complained Sima as she climbed over me into the aisle. "The movie is over." I stumbled out of my seat, feeling dizzy and cold.

On the street outside the Empire, I was stunned by the heat and the incandescence of the hot afternoon. "You really look ill. Probably got cholera. It's that season, you know."

"I can't swallow. Can't talk," I murmured to the disembodied cheery voice, which suddenly sounded like Bambi.

"You'd better go home," it said.

Shielding my eyes from the beating sun with my hand, I hailed a passing rickshaw man. He stood by, waiting to haggle over the price, but I didn't have the energy to do that. Stepping into it, I sank into the seat and was thankful for the rectangle of shade provided by the canopy. "Cook will pay," I whispered. "The address is 11 Davenport Road." He picked up the bars and started running, his feet pounding the hot macadam.

The house was empty except for Cook. I rushed to my room and flung myself on the bed. The chintz coverlet cooled my heated body. Late-afternoon sun rays on my blue-painted dresser scattered spots of light that trembled in the dusty air and seemed to dance and sway. The entire room swirled around me like a giant kaleidoscope. I floated toward the ceiling, trying to catch the shards of color. A large swarm of gnats was attacking me, and the horrendous buzzing drove me mad with pain. I tried to run away, but they surrounded me. One gnat wore a top hat and in his spindly arms he carried a black-and-white walking stick. He was poking me, and I kept pushing him away. Get away, I tried to shriek, but no words came from my mouth.

"It's Doctor Dinchess." I heard my mother's voice, as if coming from a large distance. "Let him take your temperature. You're sick." I tried to open my eyes, but they seemed stuck with some gummy material. Through a little slit, I recognized my parents leaning over my headboard. Both were frowning. A third figure standing next to them looked like a huge gnat until it came closer and I saw it was my old friend, the family doctor. He held a thermometer, which he tried to put between my puffy lips. I concentrated on opening my mouth, but nothing happened. Tears of frustration slid down my cheeks. "I can't!" I whispered.

"Doctor Dinchess came from a party. That's why he's all dressed up in black," my mother explained. Her soothing voice and Doctor Dinchess's cool hand on my hot forehead felt delicious. I started to smile but was unable to stretch my lips. Everything seemed far away and in slow motion. Someone said, "She's got scarlet fever." Another voice said, "We'll have to put her in isolation at the hospital." I floated in a giant shell filled with warm cotton wool, feeling wonderfully protected by these voices who seemed to know exactly what to do with me.

I woke up in an unfamiliar bed and in nightclothes that were itchy and smelled of chlorine. The roof of my mouth felt like caked sand. My nose itched, but when I tried to scratch it my hands seemed far away and indifferent to my wishes. A nurse appeared at my bed and was apparently talking. I saw her mouth move but heard no words. Finally I heard "scarlet fever" and "don't worry" and "You've been here two days. I am Nurse Tong." She patted my head and faded away before I had time to ask any questions.

I was frightened. May Weber, in *The Last of the Webers*, a favorite book of mine, had died of scarlet fever. I had followed May's adventures and her demise through a whole series of Weber books. In the last one there had been pages where May had "raging fevers" and "limbs contorting with pain." May had "succumbed" holding her pink chiffon scarf to her feverish brow, her last words being "Good-bye, sweet world." She was fifteen. I wept when May died, and forever after, pink chiffon reminded me of death. Now I wondered how I would die in my antiseptic white hospital gown.

I dozed off and on that day. When I had clear vision I saw that my room was small, that the walls were unadorned and painted a stark white, and that a glass of water in a chipped blue cup stood on the night table. But then everything got cloudy and the walls looked green, with wavy lines across them. The floor seemed to disassemble into little dots and dashes, all floating toward the ceiling like a tornado of flies. I kept trying to figure out these strange images and decided that maybe it depended on which eye I opened first. But before I could really figure it out, I would doze off, exhausted with the effort.

At sunset I became aware of the deep and penetrating silence in the hospital. I had been used to falling asleep in a house full of people. Nothing stirred here. I began to shiver even in the August heat. I felt the sweat matting my hair and my fingers becoming icy. A heavy-breathing monster was crouching in the shadows. It rattled and wheezed. Then it came closer. I slid under my covers, tightening myself into a little ball. Suddenly my leg touched a slimy thing. I was sure it was a snake and squeezed my legs toward my chin even tighter. I lay stiffly, not daring to move. After a while my legs cramped, but I was afraid to stretch them out. Then I heard a cough. A human cough. Three times the person coughed and then sneezed. I realized I was not alone in the hospital. Gingerly, I straightened out my cramped legs and with my left toe touched a thermometer. Relief coursed headily through my body, and I fell asleep.

My parents came to visit me, looking earnest and upset. They stood bending slightly forward, pressing their faces to the glassed-in French door. I motioned them in, but they remained behind the glass. They waved and mouthed words that I could not hear. I wondered if I had gone deaf.

"Why are my parents outside?" I screamed in terror.

Nurse Tong rushed in. "You're in quarantine. Because you are contagious. No one is allowed inside."

"What are they saying? I can't hear them."

"I told them you were a bad girl and not eating. Look, they are telling you to eat."

Vaguely I remembered someone trying to make me drink some liquid, when all I had wanted was the cool spoon in my mouth. My parents, their foreheads pressed against the French door, were mouthing, "Eat," and their breath fogged the glass. I mouthed back, "I will eat." They smiled and waved at me, then found two chairs to sit on, and for the next hour we watched each other without saying a word. I rolled up my sleeves and showed them my scarlet fever red spots, and my father said something that I could not understand.

Next day Nurse Tong told me her name was Marlena and that her Russian mother had named her after Marlene Dietrich. She said her Chinese father worked in the customshouse and that they were both very proud of her because she was a professional. She had cool hands and a soothing voice, and I loved it when she combed my matted hair into two sleek braids and put them in a crown on my head. I knew only one other Eurasian person, who was two years older than I and of such extraordinary beauty that few girls talked to her. She was always in the company of boys. Marlena Tong was also beautiful, and she was in charge at the hospital. I daydreamed of being a nurse and gliding regally and competently through long hospital corridors.

One morning I woke feeling enormously better. Like a butterfly coming out of a raggedy cocoon, my skin felt fresh and dry, and my scalp tingled. Through the French doors I looked out on a garden filled with sunflowers whose milky yellow petals bordered shiny black centers. A blue jay hopped on the veranda ledge. Pink mimosa flowers swayed in the breeze. I felt fresh and newborn and longed to go outside, but Nurse Tong said I had to be indoors a while longer. I was still in quarantine.

As strength returned, boredom set in. I waited eagerly for Nurse Tong's appearance and bombarded her with questions. Who else was in the hospital? Were there any children? Could I get dressed in my own clothes? Did she sleep in the hospital at night?

She told me she was primarily the day nurse and sometimes had night duty. The hospital had ten beds, all for contagious-disease patients, and there was only one other patient. He was a Mr. Samuel Webster, an Englishman, and he had cholera. "He was careless and ate some unwashed fruit," she told me. "These Englishmen who visit China for the first time. They think nothing will happen to them because they're British. They think they're gods." Nurse Tong obviously had a very poor opinion of the British. I certainly could not understand why any adult could be so foolish. At home I had never eaten an undoused (with permanganate) or unpeeled fruit or vegetable.

Although I was not allowed to see Mr. Webster ("Can't mix contagious diseases," said Nurse Tong), I definitely was aware of his presence. He coughed a lot. Often he called for Nurse Tong. Sometimes he cursed.

"What's he like?" I asked Nurse Tong.

"Bossy and skinny. Thinks the world revolves around him," she replied.

"Does he have visitors?"

"Hardly. He's too sick. And no family here."

"Can I see him?"

"Definitely not—you're both contagious."

"I hear him at night. He coughs a lot."

"So he does. He requires a lot of nursing, that man." I didn't tell Nurse Tong that I counted on Mr. Webster to keep the night terrors away. Every night as the hospital quieted down for the night, I continued to be assailed by visions of slimy snakes and slugs, hooded monks, and giant spiders that crept, inched, or hovered over me. Closing my eyes didn't help. Thinking of pleasant things didn't do the trick either. I waited for Mr. Webster's cough or moan. Then I would sing to myself that I was not alone at the Tientsin Contagious Disease Hospital and that nothing could hurt me. The heavy-breathing monster turned into the housecoat flung carelessly onto the chair. The hooded monk was the white curtain undulating in the night breeze.

I thought about Mr. Webster a lot. I felt there was a special bond between us, since we were the only two patients in the entire hospital.

"Does he have a wife?" I asked Nurse Tong.

"No. He's all alone. I told you that already."

"Doesn't he have anyone?" I pleaded. "Maybe I could write him a note. To cheer him up."

"Silly goose." Nurse Tong tickled me under the chin. "You're falling in love. Patients often do with each other. It's because you have so much time on your hands. And the fever. Fever always makes people fall in love."

"I'm not in love. I just want to write him a note. I have visitors every day and he has none."

Nurse Tong finally agreed to accept a note from me to Mr. Webster. "But don't sign your name. Just put 'Room #11, Children's Ward.' I don't want any hanky-panky between an eleven-year-old and a grown-up man on my shift."

She brought me some stationery with TIENTSIN CONTAGIOUS DISEASE HOSPITAL in thick black type at the top, and I wrote a note. "Dear Patient in Room 22, You and I are the only two patients in this hospital. And I hear you even though I have never seen you. Nurse Tong tells me you have no family here. I am sorry about that, because I have my parents visiting me every day. Maybe they could visit you. Yours, Patient in Room 11."

"Dear Room 11," he wrote back. "Thank you for your very sweet note. My family lives in Bath, England. Don't worry about me. Maybe we can meet when the quarantine is over for both of us. Samuel Webster."

On the fourth morning I woke up and heard Mr. Webster whistling "Rule Britannia." He kept repeating it over and over again and stopped only when he started coughing.

"Is Mr. Webster feeling better?" I asked Nurse Tong.

"He's still very sick. Actually getting worse. But he is more cheerful. Some patients get that way as they get sicker."

"Can I write to him again?"

"Why not?"

"Dear Room 22," I wrote, "I am glad you're here in the hospital with me. When I get scared at night, it's nice to know you are there. Hope you don't get scared like me. I heard you whistle 'Rule Britannia' this morning and hope you are feeling better. I am in the fifth grade at school and my favorite story is 'Heidi.' Yours, Room 11."

In the afternoon Nurse Tong brought a note from Mr. Webster. "You are having a regular love affair, you two. As long as it stays a correspondence, it's okay with me."

I didn't open the note until she left the room. I wanted to savor it by myself. "Dear Room 11. Thank you for your note. I do get scared sometimes even if I am grown-up. Everyone gets nightmares in the hospital. This is not a good place to be. I have a daughter in England who is six years old. Her name is Penelope and she lives with her mother. I like to play tennis and read mysteries. I'm glad you like my whistling. I'll try another tune if I can think of one."

During the next few days Mr. Webster and I exchanged three more notes.

"I'm getting to be a regular postal carrier," grumbled Nurse Tong, but I could see she really was not angry and actually seemed to be enjoying her role.

"Can you wheel me by his room?" I pleaded.

"Not yet. Maybe next week."

On the fifth day, after Dr. Dinchess's morning visit, Nurse Tong seemed especially cheerful. She braided red ribbons in my hair.

"I brought these for you from home," she said and hummed softly as she worked. "You remind me of my niece."

"Does she look like me?"

"No. But you're both curious, always asking questions."

"Where does she go to school?"

Nurse Tong didn't answer. She seemed suddenly to have lost interest in me. "Got to rush. Have to remind Cook about something."

My nightly terrors subsided and were replaced by dreams about Mr. Webster. But these too were disturbing. I was always being chased by bandits and followed by enormous animals. At the last moment, Mr. Webster would rush in and save me. He always wore a mask and I could never see his face.

"I bet he is good-looking," I told Nurse Tong one morning when she was combing my hair. She twined red satin ribbons in my braids.

"If you like them skinny and blond."

"I bet he has wavy hair."

"Maybe. Now it's cropped because of his high fevers."

"Does he ever ask what I look like?"

"Of course not. You're only a child. I told him how old you were."

"You didn't have to do that."

I stared at Nurse Tong and found myself hating her trim figure and gorgeous looks. As she left the room I was irritated by the swing of her buttocks. I hate Nurse Tong, I hate her, I sang under my breath. She didn't hear me. I was left alone in the room.

"Dear Room 22. I am thirteen years old and I like movies a lot. I plan to see *Gone with the Wind*. I have heard it's a great love story. I also like books written by Jules Verne. If you don't have anything to read, I could loan you my books, if Nurse Tong will let me send them to you. She is very bossy and won't let me do anything."

I decided to take this note myself to Mr. Webster. I felt bold and adventurous as I put on my new pink cotton housecoat and embroidered satin slippers. I stepped out into the hall for the first time, wondering how far Room 22 was from me. The hallway was empty. I was surprised to find Room 22 only three doors away, and then realized that the rooms were numbered at random. The door was closed. I was about to open it when Nurse Tong appeared suddenly behind me.

"Naughty child—you are not supposed to be in the corridor. Back to bed!"

Before she led me back to my room, I was able to slip my note under Mr. Webster's door.

That evening Nurse Tong brought me another note.

"Now he's initiating the correspondence. Probably is getting terribly bored."

I glared at her and put the note under my pillow. "I'll read it later."

"Dear Room 11. Got your note under the door. Aren't they allowing you to write to me? Please continue. I look forward to your notes. I am not feeling at all well tonight, so can't write much. Getting very tired."

Mr. Webster did not reply to my other notes, and Nurse Tong was noncommital about his health. "He is very tired from all the medication he is taking."

On my seventh day at the hospital Nurse Tong came in and told me Mr. Webster had died in the night. She didn't look at me as she gave me the news. Her hands were busy folding the sheets around the corners of the mattress. "Damn!" she muttered under her breath. "These linens are getting too old, don't fold nicely."

I was stunned. Nurse Tong seemed far away, and her voice sounded like the broken-down gramophone we had at home, gravelly and unclear. A huge knot appeared in my throat and I heard strange gurgling noises. The knot kept getting bigger and bigger until it filled my entire body. I realized I was sobbing.

"He died at three-fifty. He has no family, so we notified the embassy."

I couldn't imagine what the embassy would do with Mr. Webster. The only death I had known was when my kitten Archie had died. We buried him in the backyard.

"He does too have family. He had a daughter. Penelope. You have to write her. Or I have to." Tears were pouring from my eyes and my nose was stuffy.

"Stop blubbering. You'll raise your temperature. Remember, you're supposed to go home tomorrow. The embassy will handle everything."

The night after Mr. Webster died, I watched the sun set with panic. I heard the garden gate creak as the day staff left. I heard the night watchman say good night to the policeman on the corner. Nurse Tong came in to draw the curtains, and I asked if she could keep my door slightly ajar to let in some light.

"Well, it's against hospital policy. Could catch a cold with the draft." Seeing my pleading eyes, she said, "Just for tonight, because it's the first time alone in the hospital, Mr. Webster being gone. But the nightmares will soon go away, you'll see." I didn't realize she knew about my terrors and was grateful she didn't query me further about them.

She walked out of the room, leaving the door half open, and I burrowed my face into the soft pillow, hoping for instant sleep. When I couldn't breathe and hadn't fallen asleep, I turned on my side, hoping that the friendly light from the hallway would be my beacon. But the light cast strange shadows, and as my beating heart thumped wildly, I saw a tall figure dressed in white standing by the French doors. The face was covered by a hood, and it was swaying. I ordered myself to close my eyes, but they seemed transfixed on this strange creature. My heart now was galloping with loud, irregular thumps, and sweat oozed down my forehead into my eyes and mouth and I could taste its saltiness. The figure kept swaying and appeared to be moving toward me.

Suddenly I heard a moan. Then a cough. Then laughter. Mr. Webster, I thought. Mr. Webster is here and will dissolve my terrors. Then I remembered Mr. Webster was dead, and a new fear gripped me. Where were the noises coming from? Was this Mr. Webster's ghost? Was he angry with me for not visiting him? Who was making the noises? Perhaps a killer who had snuck into the hospital past the night watchman. The noises were increasing and seemed quite close. I heard more moans. Then I heard laughter and giggles. Then an *ah* . . . and an *oh* . . . I heard Nurse Tong's voice say, "Shh . . . quiet, the child is still here," and a male voice say, "Oh, Marlena . . ." There were more muffled moans, squeals, then quiet. Total quiet. I fell asleep.

"Still having nightmares?" Nurse Tong asked next morning as she pulled the curtains apart. I looked out on a dazzling new day. "You'll be going home today."

"I heard noises last night. Moans . . . and even laughter."

Nurse Tong was efficiently folding the blankets. "Your imagination again. Mr. Webster is dead, so there are no noises now. You are the only patient here."

"But . . ."

"I promise you. When you go back home, you will not remember the nightmares. Or the noises. You will forget everything. I command you . . . as your superior officer." She gave me a mock salute and sailed out of the room.

My parents came in the morning to pick me up. We sat for the last time in the hospital garden on the bench beneath the mimosa tree. I was surprised at my sadness in leaving. My room looked so peaceful and cozy. My father handed me several get well cards from classmates. "Read them," he said cheerily. "They all want you back."

I looked at the first one, from Brenda, who had written, "Roses are red, violets are blue, get well soon and I'll see you." Tom's card said, "Violets are blue, roses are red, come back soon or I'll be sed (ha! ha!)." Sima had scrawled, "See ya at the movies." I found myself thinking that the cards were silly and childish and that I would have a hard time thanking them. I couldn't even remember their faces. I tried to conjure them up, but nothing came. My mind remained blank.

"Don't you like them?" my mother's voice wafted into my reverie.

"I guess so."

My parents didn't seem to hear me. They were packing my clothes into the black valise we always took with us on trips and saying good-bye to Nurse Tong. They thanked her for her good care of me and presented her with an envelope, which she tucked into her pocket. She waved to me as we walked out of the garden into the streets, and I wondered what she would do now, since there were no patients left at the Tientsin Contagious Disease Hospital.

When I went back to school the following week, I was greeted with a bunch of yellow daisies and a giant heart-shaped card with everyone's signature, including that of my teacher, Mrs. Matson. She asked me to come before the class and share my experiences of being in a hospital.

"Well," I said, "it was really interesting. I was the only patient. They gave me gallons of ice cream for my throat, and the nurse brought me all sorts of reading material."

I got bolder with every word, feeling a thrilling new power as I looked at the rapt faces in front of me. I told them I was allowed to walk all over the hospital and even watched an operation once.

"Boy, what an adventure!" Tom said with envy and asked me if I would like to borrow his Jules Verne books.

I didn't tell them about the terrors. Nor about the nightmares at home, or the light I slept with in my bedroom since my return from the hospital. I didn't tell them about the strange noises I had heard my last night in the hospital, or about Mr. Webster.

I looked at their faces, and they seemed familiar and strange to me. Tom, with his shock of red hair, looked silly in knee pants. I could see his scratched, knobby knees. Brenda's tight pigtails looked childish. I felt different from them. It was as if a wall had sprung up between us, a glass wall where the images were unfocused. In my body I felt a thrusting feeling, as if my bones were stretching out and pushing my skin beyond its boundaries. "Growing pains," my mother had told me when I described them. That pain was frightening and delicious at the same time. "Are you dizzy?" asked Mrs. Matson. "This is your first day back. Maybe you ought to lie down. You look shaky."

The recess bell rang. Everyone jumped up and ran toward the door. I watched as they all scuffled madly to be the first one out.

"Are you coming?"

"Soon. I'll come later."

I waited until the room was empty and then slowly walked out.

Opaque Windows

WHEN I BECAME twelve, I was allowed to spend time in Tientsin's Victoria Park by myself. Previously I had been rigorously attended by amahs and governesses, who hovered over my every move. On my first solitary outing, I walked warily toward the park, scanning the ground for troublesome pebbles, avoiding contact with all fearsome things. I headed straight toward my favorite swing, protected by the shade of a deeply bent weeping willow tree. While in the ecstasy of high swings, one of my shoes fell off. It was picked up by a woman with bright orange curls topped by a tiny black straw hat. What stunned me most was her one short leg and the massive wooden heel it rested on. She handed me my lost shoe full of sand as I stared at her obscene one, and for a moment our glances held. I quickly looked away when she hobbled off, her body grinding and swaying as she maneuvered back to her seat on the bench in front of the red pagoda. I put my shoe on and avoided looking at her. Out of the corner of my eye, though, I saw that she sat silently amid a group of chattering Chinese amahs. Later, I found in my shoe a battered business card that read, "Madame Dubois. Giver of French Lessons. Experienced. 12 Hang-chu Lane."

I stuck the card in my sweater pocket. It was later discovered by my mother, who claimed it was fate because she had just been thinking of sending me off for French lessons and wasn't it wonderful and ingenious that Madame Dubois had stuck her card in my shoe. "She's teaching the Gintz children, and Mrs. Gintz says they're speaking French already," said my mother. My father said, "Damn good advertising technique. That woman is a born saleswoman."

"But she is . . . lame," I stumbled over the word. Having been born with a congenital hip problem, I was aware that the word "lame" had been obliterated from our vocabulary. I was amazed I even said it.

My parents exchanged glances. "She just has a little walking difficulty," cooed my mother. "And an excellent reputation as a teacher."

"Probably tired the day you saw her," offered my father.

"And that hair of hers—what a glorious color!" my mother's voice caressed.

"Titian red! A great painter, Titian. I'll get his work from the library," said my father, as we dexterously skirted the issue.

My panic about Madame Dubois remained an immensity that could not be reached or touched but that swirled around me like viperous fumes. I would go to the first lesson like an obedient calf, because somewhere in me resided an instinct that knew I had to conquer terrors, that overcoming them was good. Hadn't my parents always told me that there was nothing I could not do? I went because they wanted me to go. Even if they had stopped having answers for me, I loved them incomparably, although I was beginning to think of them as charming older children in whose care I had been haphazardly placed.

With my mother, I arrived at 12 Hangchu Lane one afternoon in early August when the summer *fu-tiens* smothered my town like a heavy woolen shroud, when not a breath stirred and even the birds seemed stunned into songlessness by the relentless heat. I oozed dampness and my brain felt addled and I yearned for the coolness of marble, for swimming pools, the Alps, and floating Arctic icebergs. The run-down brick building before us looked like a factory.

"Are you sure this is the place?" I quizzed my mother, who somehow was always able to look cool and unwrinkled.

"Of course."

"How do you know?"

"I called ahead. From your father's office," she explained—we did not have a phone.

"But this doesn't look like a place . . . for lessons."

"Well, sometimes things don't look like what they are supposed to. Who would have thought a French teacher would be scouring the parks for pupils? Weren't we lucky?" she said brightly. "Pick you up later. Go ahead. You can do it. You're growing up."

I was not reassured and was convinced that either my mother had misread the battered business card or the teacher had given her wrong directions. The house looked evil and forbidding. My mother nudged me toward the door, waved to me gaily, and left me staring at a long, rickety, unswept stairway. At the corner she waved me on again.

The stairs creaked at every step. I was hoping that with all this noise someone would meet me at the top, but no one appeared. Instead, as I proceeded cautiously skyward, a sound of humming and buzzing began to fill my ears, growing louder with each step, and I became convinced that I was nearing a behemoth angry beehive, but now there was no turning back.

I crossed the threshold into a brightly lit room with numerous sewing machines surrounded by bolts of multicolored yarn and cloth, bins filled with threads, buttons, and lace, and a floor littered with gossamery iridescent cloth fuzz. A Chinese girl bent over each sewing machine. A martinet Chinese man marched around the room, blowing rings of smoke from his dangling cigarette holder. He yanked the pigtails of the workers in order to get their attention, poking his bony fingers at mistakes in the garments. When one of them turned her head my way, I was shocked to see that she was only a little older than I. Centuries of instilled wariness and suspicion prevented us from looking into each other's eyes. Except for the hum of the machines, there was no sound but the stillness of merciless, boring labor, the soundlessness of despair.

Madame Dubois, dressed in a heavy black cape that made me sweat just looking at it, beckoned to me from the doorway. Her room was small and dingy, with peeling walls and a window so spotted with dust and festooned with lacy cobwebs that the outside world looked milky and out of focus. I couldn't recognize my town at all. A small bird of panic nested in me. Where was I?

She dusted off a grimy chair, raising a cloud of gray powder that settled like black-hearted rain on my damp body. I felt a dis-ease, a disjointedness, a discomfort. Later I would wonder why Madame had made no effort to improve her surroundings. Was she flaunting the dust, the seediness, the grime in order to draw attention to her miserable milieu and hike her prices up? Had she, like my parents, trained herself to be immune to disagreeableness, to seek the protective comfort of opaque vision? Or was she totally mad? Had this strange, exotic, harsh land knocked all the adults senseless?

Our first lesson went by uneventfully. I conjugated verbs and read a story. She corrected my pronunciation. Periodically she got up to roam around the room, clanking and dragging her monstrous shoe behind her. She moved like a wounded, caged lion, sniffing the dust, pawing her mis-shapen boot as if in pain. Her heavy cape swung around her as if there were a wind, but it was suffocatingly still in the room. I sweated. She was dry as a bleached bone.

"Well, I told you this was the place," said my mother cheerily when she picked me up. "Did you like it? I hear she is a good teacher."

"Well, I don't know. Yet. But her room is . . . so awful. Filled with dust," I said cautiously.

"She's a widow, you know. Ekes out a living by giving lessons. I'm sure you'll be fine," Mother warbled merrily. Gently pulling me by the hand, she led me across the street. This was no time for fears.

Once a week I climbed the creaking stairs to Madame's barren room, past the low-bent heads of the children, through the sea of colorful fluff that clung to my shoes and socks like spiky dandelions. Usually Madame was hunched over her hot plate, and I smelled burnt onions and liver, which made me gag.

I asked Madame if she knew the children in the big room. "What children? They are young women."

"But do you know them?"

"Of course not. They are at work. One is not to be disturbed when one is working. And now it is time for you to work."

November arrived early on wings of chill winds. I wore layers of cloth-ing, but Madame never changed her attire and seemed to be totally im-mune to meteorologic variations. She began to collect plants, and for a few weeks her room bloomed with the strange profusion of growths. She said they were a gift from her friend who worked in the mortuary and who took home all the leftover flowering plants from funerals and weddings. She murmured, "Ah, I forgot to water my babies again. I will have to buy a watering can." But the flowers continued to droop, and no watering can appeared.

One day I arrived and found Madame at her hot plate with her back to the door. The flowers were in various stages of decay, the earth around them bleached dry. I sat down at the desk waiting for her to join me. I hoped she had totally forgotten about the lesson and would never turn around and I could, after a few minutes, slip quietly away unnoticed. Suddenly she turned abruptly toward me and hobbled to her bed. She slowly unlaced the black shoestrings and took off her shoes and socks. I watched in horror as the monstrous shoe fell to the floor with a thud. This was the first time I had seen her feet without shoes. They looked disappointingly normal, except that one leg was at least eight inches shorter than the other. I had expected a deformed monstrosity, imagining clubfeet with hooves, webbed toes, taloned claws. Here were two delicate and perfectly formed feet, the skin milky-cream. She lay still, not paying any attention to me. Then she began to twitch and pulsate. The bed swayed from side to side. Was this an earthquake?

Suddenly sobs crescendoed out of her into explosive cries and inhuman howls that came from some volcanic pit. Sounds streamed out of Madame in a torrential lava flash, French words rolled out like gravelly pebbles.

"*Mon anniversaire*. This is my anniversary. Wedding anniversary. Would have been married thirty-five years. Oh, he was so *joli*, so loving, such a fine figure. Wore such elegant clothes and had magnificent feet. Not a blemish on them. So white, so perfect, the toenails so pink. Both of them so perfect. And when he joined the French army and wore his uniform he was so, so . . ." Madame bolted straight up in bed as if a puppeteer had jerked her string abruptly. "So handsome, so debonair, so *magnifique*. I adored him. *Je t'adore*," she moaned.

I stared at this outburst, trying to follow the *rat-a-tat* French words. Wanting to evaporate into mist, I felt trapped. Madame leaned toward me, beckoning me closer with her bony finger, and whispered, "Would you like to see my husband—*mon mari*?"

I nodded yes, and she slid down the bed and dove underneath, leaving only her rear end sticking out like a giant black balloon suspended in air. I stared hopelessly through the opaque window trying to make out the shape of the world outside, resigning myself to photo albums, probably all faded and smudged. I would be polite, as I had been taught. I would look. When she finally emerged, she was gripping a dusty wooden box in her hands. With both hands outstretched, she presented the box to me as if it were the crown jewels and she the royal queen.

"*C'est mon mari*," she said tenderly, but a bat in me squeaked with terror. I shied away. "You do not want to hold it?" she sighed and then slowly opened the filthy box top. Inside was sandy dirt. It smelled musty, unaired, old, sinister in its very ordinariness.

Madame swayed back and forth, holding the box to her bosom and moaning softly to herself. "They shot," she whispered conspiratorially to me, her eyes filling with tears. "They shot him because they said he smuggled arms to the other side. To the other side," she whispered knowingly, coming closer to me and looking around as if there were enemy ears straining to hear her. "I was at the execution. They made me watch. He and several others were shot. *Piff-paff.* With their hands tied behind their back. *Piff-paff.* And then they threw them all in a ditch. I pleaded to have Pierre's body, but they said no and they burned them all. Later that night I returned and filled this box with his ashes. *Mon pauvre* Pierre has kept me company all these years." She continued rocking, nursing the box, caressing it with her cheek.

Then Madame lay back on the bed and took the pins out of her hair, letting the flaming red curls slide down her back. The hair spread around her like a halo. She closed her eyes and fell asleep. I left quietly, creeping past the bent black heads of the sewing girls, who did not stir as I went by. The thought of telling my parents about this incident flitted like a butterfly through my mind, but I brushed it away. Even though their night quarrels had increased, they had few answers and required a problem-free world. As always, cheery days followed stormy nights as if nothing had happened. They were sure that I saw only the dazzle of daylight. No need to upset their vision with my tale of Madame.

That December the town was coated with short-lived snow, which for a few days softened and muffled its voice. Madame's coal stove sputtered anxiously but produced a puny heat. We conjugated verbs and read out of an ancient French geography book, totally outdated. She appeared listless, mumbling, "*Très bien, très bien,*" but the words sounded hollow and empty. She didn't seem to notice at all one day when I switched books and began to read one of my English books. She stared blankly and bit her lips until they bled. She no longer cooked her vile liver concoctions and did not make any attempt to wipe off the dusty chair. The plants were fully dead now, bent over their pots like exhausted ballerinas. Madame sat and stared, her brow furrowed, at the ice-encrusted window, as if trying to decipher some secret code, looking for a sign, waiting for an overdue message. One day I recited some poems in Russian, but she never batted an eye, never changed her stare or her position by the window. Languages had lost their boundaries for her, had become indistinguishable.

During the next months Madame began to look like a punctured air bag slowly leaking gas, shriveled, wrinkled, and lifeless. The lacy cobwebs hung in corners. The dust mounted on the desk, and even though pink-petaled spring arrived, Madame remained shrouded in her heavy black coat. At the end of June my mother received a garish Christmas card depicting a Christ who looked distinctly Chinese. Madame Dubois had scrawled on the back, "Have to give up lessons. Family matters." And my mother said, "Well, that's that! We'll have to find a new teacher. How about the summer off? It will give you time to practice your swimming."

I danced around my mother with great joy and almost knocked her over.

"It wasn't all that bad, was it?" she asked pleadingly.

"No, it was fine, just fine. I'm just glad it's summer," I lied.

I spent the next months in the city swimming pool, coming out after hours of immersion with fingers and toes puckered like shriveled claws. Staring at the summer sun, I thought of Madame and wondered what she was doing. I wondered how the sewing girls were, surrounded by the debris of threads and cloth that no doubt was sticking to their skin. And the stern overseer—was he adding to the heat of the room with plumes of cigarette smoke?

A few months later I saw Madame Dubois again. She was sitting on the bench near the red pagoda in Victoria Park where I had first met her. I went up to her, but she did not acknowledge me. She was looking at some internal landscape and smiling as she hugged the wooden box close to her body, cooing to it. I watched as she got up, walked around the bench, and emptied the box of its contents. She knelt and began to dig for more earth, which she put into the box. "The ashes are getting old and stale . . . and Pierre was so young. Perhaps it really is not Pierre—there were three shot that day," she muttered under her breath. I watched in horror as she not only refilled the box but delicately ate some of the dirt, smacking her lips with relish.

Many years later I was in an antique shop in Paris. It was a rain-pelting day with mists swirling, and through the shop window I saw a world diffused and soft, like Monet's paintings. Among the tumble of bric-a-brac, nestled between a Tiffany vase and a silver butter knife, I saw a little statue of the three monkeys who Spoke No Evil, Saw No Evil, and Heard No Evil. Substitute "sorrow" for "evil." Suddenly I realized that was my family. Bound together, living lives of unreported and unacknowledged woe. A heavy heart was not to be tolerated. My parents, alive and active, still clinging to the idea that this was the best of all possible worlds. They had passed on to me an incomparably defiant will and the ability to see beauty in the smallest raindrop or most ordinary cloud. Silently I thanked them for this rare gift.

Holding the statuette, now warm and moist in my hands, I looked out of the steamy window. I saw a woman hobbling. She wore a black cape and had red hair. My heart stopped. Madame! Madame Dubois! I silently screamed. I ran after her into the rain, but she had melted into the mist and I realized that if she were alive she would be more than a hundred years old.

Forgive me, I whispered, for not understanding your suffering. And for not reporting it. I didn't know how. I was not allowed. They wanted me to see a world filled with sunshine and open windows. And yours were always so opaque.

There was a lightness in me as I walked back to the shop. "May I have this, please?" I asked in impeccable French, pointing to the statuette in the palm of my hand.

Pei-tai-ho Summers

THE AUGUST RAINS ping and steady-spatter on the roof of the lacy gazebo, but we are cozily huddled in the center and do not mind because we are concentrating on playing Monopoly. We are wet with perspiration and the occasional gusty raindrops that zigzag drunkenly our way, but the game continues. Hunched over the board, we buy, sell, make avaricious deals. We ignore the calls of parents wanting us to come in for dinner and later protest that it was impossible to hear anything over the rainy din, the thunderclaps and flashes of lightning. But of course we hear them.

Every summer we come here for three months, languishing all winter for the miles of velvety white sands, dreaming of the jagged joining of churning water and sand and the white-plumed linking of water and granite. This last summer in Pei-tai-ho on the Yellow Sea we live in a compound of six bungalows, each with five or six rooms and a common dining room. Every bungalow has a wraparound veranda with identical wicker furniture and slippery chintz-covered pillows that slide whenever I try to prop myself on them. Each room is occupied by a mother and children, the fathers arriving only on weekends. Our voices are raucous with summer freedom in our veins, and there is no quieting us. Servants, who live in the back of each bungalow, bring us milk, sandwiches with the bread edges cut off, and piles of oranges from Florida.

At Pei-tai-ho beach with my father.

When the sun comes out, brushing everything with diamond glitter, we run to the beach, towels flying in the wind, arms full of rubber rafts and bags of toys. We ignore maternal voices yelling, "Not so fast!" "You haven't finished your food!" "Don't forget to wear your hat." We tell them later that we were too far away to hear. Their voices do not carry, we say. We relish the sight of them running after us, struggling to keep up. Some mothers carry sandwiches with them; others, piles of extra towels; some, bags of oranges. Every day the Chinese beach peddler sells dolls made out of flour and water, molding them in front of us and painting them in bright colors. He tries to interest us in them, but we pretend to sleep and ignore him.

By the end of August we are all as brown and glossy as lichee nuts. We have been at the beach every day, and every day the Yellow Sea surprises us with different faces. There is the churning, big-wave, "I'll eat you up" face; the delicate, lacy wavelets-tickling-our-toes face; the smooth-as-glass face. We are proud of having skillfully avoided our parents most of the time and look forward to next year—only nine months away.

With friends at Pei-tai-ho beach.

We never come back. War, occupation keep us from moving out of town and the summers in Pei-tai-ho fade away into the deep recesses of our minds, occasionally brought out with "Do you remember the silky sand?" or "Do you remember the piles of oranges?" We sigh, blink, stare off into space, and never forget.

The Pursuit of Music

LUDMILLA PETROVNA HOHLACHKIN was my piano teacher from the time I was five years old. A tall, stately Russian woman, with hair piled high on top of her head, she always wore lacy blouses with a cameo brooch at the throat. She reminded me of the pictures of the czarina. Her eyes looked fevered, and the two spots on her cheeks turned bright red when she got excited. It was rumored that there had been a husband who had left her, an abortionist now living with a Eurasian. She never spoke of him. Our life was totally dedicated to the pursuit of music.

She lived with her sister in a small two-room apartment on the fourth floor of a moldy gray apartment house. The tiny living room was overpowered by two pianos standing at an angle and two lumpy, overstuffed couches. A brooding portrait of Beethoven, his forehead furrowed deeply in despair, dominated the walls. Two dogs, Leda and Nero, shared these cramped quarters. During my lessons I would hear them pacing in the hallway, thumping their tails.

Ludmilla Petrovna did not believe in the interruption of lessons and did not acknowledge holidays or vacations. We met twice weekly, Tuesdays and Fridays. During the hot summer months when we were not in Pei-tai-ho, the unpaved alley behind the apartment house smelled of rotten vegetables spilling out of the rows of garbage cans. Around the corner was a fish market, and on particularly hot, steamy days the mixture of these smells followed me up to the fourth floor, subsiding only when Ludmilla Petrovna quickly shut the door behind me. During the winter months the apartment was penetratingly cold. From November to March I played the piano in cut-off gloves to keep my fingers warm and did not take off my coat. She sat wrapped in an afghan shawl, stiff and majestic, swinging her arms like a conductor and counting out loud. With determination, we marched through all the seasons, impervious to heat or cold, disregarding discomfort, pouring our energies into the teaching and learning of music. I was under her spell.

Ludmilla Petrovna had studied with Paderewski at the St. Petersburg conservatory, and now she dreamt of a brilliant musical career for me. She demanded complete devotion to her art, hours of practice, a flawless technique, and playing "with the soul." Toward the attainment of this perfection, she told me that my fingers were "little soldiers" and had to be regimented and disciplined. She made me play the scales with a matchbox tethered to my hand, so that if I swerved and the box fell she would not lose time retrieving it. As I advanced, the umbilical string was severed and my "little soldiers" performed faultlessly without the box. "Feel, feel, when you play," she said. "Be soft as a butterfly and firm as a soldier. And practice. Always practice. At least two hours every single day. Always, and you will go far." My chest expanded with delight. I loved pleasing her and submitted cheerfully to her regimen.

But as I grew into puberty, strange new feelings began to invade my being. Calls of the heart, rumblings of a budding sexuality preoccupied me, and I found the unrelenting practice of piano a chore. I needed time to savor new discoveries. One day I pleaded tearfully to change our routine—to come once a week instead of twice—to practice one hour a day instead of two. Ludmilla Petrovna stood up from her chair, swayed as if on unsteady feet, and stared at me as if I were a traitor. "To music you have to give all. There is no other way. Music cannot be done halfway." I pleaded and cried, but she remained firm. There was to be no compromise. After a nine-year relationship, she told me to leave and never to return. I left the brooding Beethoven, Leda and Nero thumping their tails, the unheated stove, the tiny apartment. Her sister smiled at me weakly at the door but didn't say anything. There was no arguing with the indomitable Ludmilla Petrovna. We both knew it.

Many of her other pupils had already left her because of her uncompromising demands. She remained compulsively true to her ideals. The sister tried to augment their declining income by taking in sewing, but she was not successful and they hovered on the edge of poverty for several years. When I left China in 1948 I did not have the courage to go to say good-bye. By then I knew that I had failed her and couldn't make up for it. I learned much later that she died in 1950 of TB; the feverish spots on her cheeks had consumed her.

Ludmilla Petrovna has always dwelt in me. She left her imprint so categorically that even without her presence I continue to follow her regimen and live by her precepts. I have craved discipline with tenacity and passion. It has been the bulwark of my life, the thing I can always count on. I comfort myself with its shape. And I have thrilled to the continual flexing of my soul, exalting in the softness of butterflies and the dreaminess of imagination.

"We Must Return the Hospitality"

LOOKING AT ME with her serious brown eyes, beneath the brows that formed a single line across her forehead, she said, "No, we can't have Shirley Canberry in our house for the afternoon." We were sitting, my mother and I, on the second-floor veranda of Grandmother's house—the house we shared with relatives and several other families—and I was rhythmically kicking the leg of the bamboo chair as I listened to her. She was wearing my favorite dress, the yellow cotton with black polka dots and the sewn-in black cummerbund that circled her tiny waist—a waist that I yearned to have someday, though mine now was at the dumpy, preadolescent, twelve-year-old stage. It was May, but the air was still gritty with leftover Gobi Desert March dust and I could feel the sand in my mouth as I licked my dry lips. Through the veranda railing I could see Cook, tall with bulging biceps ("unusual build for a North Chinese," my mother often said), throwing out the evening garbage into the two huge metal bins by the kitchen. Sui, the houseboy, was leaning against a tree, smoking a cigarette, drawing in the smoke in great gulps and then slowly emitting it in delicate rings. The rickshaw boy, Woo, was squatting on the ground and eating his rice from a bowl. He looked up and waved, and I waved back. I could hear their conversation but could understand only a few words in Chinese, because although I had been born here, I did not speak Chinese; I spoke Russian at home and English in school.

"But why can't Shirley come to the house?" I insisted.

My mother sighed and looked past me. There was a long silence as she gazed off into the distance and I kept kicking the chair, unraveling the rattan cords that bound the leg, leaving them in a wiry puddle on the floor.

"Because we don't have a house like the Canberrys'. Shirley would be uncomfortable here. She's an embassy child. We have only one bathroom, and there are . . ." Mother counted to herself, "at least eight people on the second floor sharing it."

"Shirley doesn't care about bathrooms," I said.

"Well, how many do the Canberrys have?"

I looked at her, thinking this was ridiculous, but realized she really was serious and expected an answer. "They have four."

"You see," said my mother triumphantly. "I tell you it won't work to have her here. We'll take her to Victoria Cafe for tea." She leaned back into her high-backed rattan chair, plumped the blue chintz pillows behind her, and began to read a book.

I continued, "Let's forget the whole thing. I'll just keep going over to the Canberrys', and she doesn't have to go anywhere with us."

The thought of spending an afternoon at Victoria Cafe, dressed to the teeth, having to mind my manners and listen to the quartet of four elderly German-Jewish refugees playing old-fashioned Viennese waltzes made me squirm with embarrassment. I knew Shirley would hate it. She hated being cooped up inside and getting dressed up. Shirley and I had discovered the joys of taking long walks and were often absent for hours from the Canberry household, wandering in the Chinese quarters—a fact I kept from my parents, who had always warned me never to leave the European concessions. But Mrs. Canberry didn't seem to mind at all and actually encouraged us to "discover" the world. She often told me how lucky I was to be living here and how she hoped Shirley would "absorb" all the wonders of China before they had to go home to the States on home leave. Shirley and I would go down Victoria Road, cross the bridge to the Italian concession, and then find ourselves in the Chinese part of town, where the streets were narrow and spilling over with merchants hawking their wares. Wash hung from the balconies, and little children ran around merrily. The smells of unwashed linens, feces, and cooked rice, the bustle of people milling around, excited and frightened me at the same time. Feeling overwhelmed by the sights and sounds, I often wanted to go back before

Shirley was ready. "Can't figure you out," Shirley would say. "You're so un-comfortable here in your own country. I love being in the States." I was usually silent, since I could not explain my discomfort and envied her cocksureness, her matter-of-factness, while I floundered in my uncer-tainty. Did I love my homeland, did I hate it? I didn't really know. All I knew was that I adored Shirley and wanted to be just like her.

My mother interrupted my thoughts. "We have to do it—because we have to return the hospitality. You keep going over to the Canberrys' all the time, and we have never entertained Shirley."

"But I know she doesn't like going to cafes."

"Well, it will be a new experience for her."

"Why can't I just bring something to the Canberrys? To return the hos-pitality, I mean. Something for Mrs. Canberry."

My mother perked up at this idea, and I could see her giving it some thought. I watched her as she wrinkled her nose and concentrated. "No, I don't think that would work," she finally said. "If you give something to Mrs. Canberry, she would then have to give you something in return and then we would have to—no. I don't think it would work."

"But you exchange gifts with the Dridens."

"That's different."

"Why?"

"Because it is. Let's not argue. Invite Shirley. We'll go to the Victoria for ice cream and cake. Saturday at four o'clock."

"Well, at least they have adequate bathroom facilities there," I said as I flounced out of my chair, giving the bamboo chair a swift kick, and ran downstairs into the garden.

The garden was overgrown with weeds. I sat underneath my favorite weeping willow tree and stared up at my mother, who was reading her book. She looked cool and lemony in her yellow dress, and I felt hot and itchy. I heard the veranda door creak and saw my aunt come out and join her. I could hear them laughing together.

I pressed my back into the trunk of the willow as I squatted at its base, picking a few daisies and making a chain out of them. "Don't lean against the tree, you'll tear your dress," I heard my mother say as she leaned on the veranda rail and looked down at me. I pressed even deeper into the bark, squashing my white linen blouse against it and hoping it would leave huge unwashable stains down the back. "Come in, come in, it's getting dark," I heard her say, and her voice seemed to be coming from a great distance as the sun set and evening breezes cooled the dusty garden.

I couldn't figure out a way to tell Shirley about the Victoria Cafe plan in a diplomatic manner when I saw her the next day in school, so I just blurted it out. "We're going to the Victoria for tea. You and me and my mother." Shirley stared at me with her protruding blue eyes beneath the fashionably cut bangs and didn't say anything. "Just you and me and my mother," I repeated furiously.

"I hate the Victoria," said Shirley. "You know how I hate getting dressed up. Besides, none of the embassy people ever go there."

"My mother says we have to return the hospitality. I'm always going over to your house."

"So what? My mother likes having you over."

"I know. But it's uneven. Me always going to your place."

"Why do you always have to compare? Let's just have fun."

I looked at Shirley, who was drawing pictures on the ground with a branch, weaving an intricate pattern of circles and crosses. Shirley was always talking about having fun and chastising me for being too serious, and I wondered if one had to be an American to reach that wonderful state, but such thoughts always led me to desperation, since I knew I would never be an American and therefore would never achieve that delicious state of "fun" that Shirley always talked about.

"I think you should come to Victoria Cafe. Otherwise my mother will keep after me. Or she might even not let me go to your house anymore."

Shirley rolled her eyes with an expression that said "grown-ups—they are impossible" and agreed to meet us on Saturday. "How will you get there?" I asked.

"I'll have the chauffeur drive me—it's too far to walk and I'm sure Daddy will let me use the embassy car on a weekend if I ask him."

We didn't speak of the impending Saturday date during the next week, although we saw each other daily at school. On Thursday, as we did every week during the warm months, we "camped" in the Canberry backyard, sleeping under a tent that was set up by the Chinese servants the night before and lying on sleeping bags that the family had brought from the States. Shirley always told me stories of how her family spent summers in

the Colorado Rockies, the Grand Canyon, and Yosemite, and my mind
would whirl with visions of giant waterfalls, soaring snowcapped mountains, and prowling bears. "Sleeping on the ground," as my mother called
camping, was considered a strange American aberration, leading to colds
and backaches, but after much pleading, I was allowed to indulge in this
pastime with Shirley.

That evening we sat in front of the tent by a small campfire that had
been lit for us and roasted marshmallows on a branch cut to size by the
Canberrys' number one houseboy, Liu. "I like sleeping under the stars,
don't you?" said Shirley. "I just can't wait till we get back to the States and
do some real camping, not just backyard camping. Maybe you could come
and visit. Do you think your parents would let you? It would be such fun."

"Sure, Shirl," I said, knowing full well that none of this would come to
pass. "Sure, I'll come and visit."

"Super," said Shirley as we snuggled into our sleeping bags and went
to sleep.

I woke early on Saturday morning and heard the chattering of the servants outside my window. Under the walkway that connected the house
to the kitchen I saw Cook sitting on the barber's chair having his shiny
bald head scrubbed vigorously by the traveling barber, who came around
every few weeks to shave people and cut hair. Cook's wife was squatting
on the ground eating her morning bowl of noodles, and his two children
were throwing smooth, shiny pebbles into a can. The streets were empty
at this early hour.

My mother called me and said that this was the day we were going to
meet Shirley at the Victoria, and I made a face at myself in the mirror and
mouthed, "As if I could ever forget." She bustled around me all morning,
making sure I washed my hair and set it in curlers. She had my yellow
dress ironed by Cook's wife and fussed around in my chest of drawers trying to find just the exact shade of socks to match the dress. She even had
my hair ribbon starched and ironed.

"Why this preparation? Shirley will probably come in her overalls—the
ones she just got from the States."

"You know that everyone dresses for the Victoria."

"Everyone except Shirley. She hates the Victoria."

"I'm sure her mother will have her wear a dress."

"Her parents are away this weekend. There's just her older sister and Kent, her brother."

Throughout the day I wandered around the house feeling restless. I went downstairs to watch Cook prepare for the midday meal. He was chopping vegetables with the big cleaver, and a cigarette dangled in his mouth. I watched as the ash collected on the butt and hung over the carrots and onions. Just as it was about to fall, he flicked it off with a powerful jerk. Cook's children were squatting on the ground drawing pictures in the sand, and I squatted down with them for a few minutes, but they seemed disinterested in me and I walked off. I went inside and knocked on Mary's door on the ground floor. She opened it and stood silhouetted in the doorway, her eyes filled with tears and her tangled hair a halo around her head. "My mother is after me," she muttered. "I can't talk to you now." And she slammed the door in my face and left me alone in the hallway. I knocked on Mrs. Miller's door, and hearing no answer, I peeked in and saw her sleeping on the couch, her enormous body covered by an afghan that had slipped halfway down to the floor. She was snoring loudly, each snore an elaborate cacophony of gurgles and wheezes. I closed the door and went upstairs, where I lay down and picked up *A Tale of Two Cities* to read while I waited for four o'clock to come.

I must have fallen asleep because my mother was yelling at me to get up and telling me it was late and we would never get to the Victoria on time. At three-thirty, I, in my yellow dress with socks to match, and she, in a blue silk dress with puffy sleeves and shoes to match, were on our way, rushing through the streets and not stopping to talk to anyone, just saying "Hello—we're on our way to the Victoria" to people we passed.

"She's here already and we've made her wait," said my mother as we turned the corner of Davenport and Victoria Road and saw Shirley standing by the front door of the Victoria. She was leaning casually against the door, both her hands on her hips, and looking around with a bored expression. She was dressed in an elegant sailor-suit outfit of the sort that was popular that year, and my mother said, "I told you she would get dressed up." I didn't answer her.

Inside the Victoria I could smell the freshly baked goods that were arranged on white doilies in the shiny glass counters. Presiding over the bakery was the owner, a lady as round and fresh as her crescent breads,

with beady, raisin-black eyes embedded in her fleshy face. She greeted us
in a husky voice, panting with every word as she lumbered around in her
sensible shoes. From the homey domain of the bakery, we moved on to
the interior of the Victoria, the cafe itself, where everything was somber
and heavy. There were no windows, and the big room was lit by wall
sconces and hanging chandeliers. Only years later would I understand the
comfort of a darkened room in the middle of the afternoon. At the time
I felt oppressed by the brocaded wall coverings and the black leather
booths lining the walls and the thick carpet under my feet that scratched
my open-toed sandals. There were several scattered tables with shiny
tablecloths in the middle of the room, and as my eyes became accustomed
to the dimness the quartet of musicians swam into my vision. We sat down
at a table close to them, and they began to play "On the Beautiful Blue
Danube," a Strauss waltz. My mother settled with a contented sigh into
her chair, and Shirley looked at me and rolled her eyes.

There were few people in the room at this time of day, and soon a waiter
appeared and we gave our order. Shirley looked bored and couldn't decide
what to order, and my mother spent a long time going over the menu with
her. Finally a decision was made to have an American Sundae, a concoction of ice creams, bananas, and chocolate cookies topped by whipped
cream and mandarin oranges that was always a favorite of mine. We also
ordered "kuchkas," a mound of chocolate melted into wafers and stacked
in a triangular shape, which Shirley always insisted was "just cornflakes
and melted chocolate." She could never see why I got so excited about it.

The quartet was now playing "Sounds from the Vienna Woods," and
my mother was swaying with the music and tapping her feet to the one-
two-three. She waved to Mr. Berman the violinist, who nodded to her
without missing a beat. He played at numerous functions around town
and was known to have been a member of the Berlin Philharmonic before
the war. Now he gave lessons and played at the Victoria. I watched Shirley
as she dug into her American Sundae, picking out the cookies and laying
them aside as prizes to be eaten later.

My mother was asking Shirley about the States, and Shirley was answering politely and even with enthusiasm. I saw Shirley in a new light as
I listened to her talk with pride about her hometown in Illinois. She said
they would be going home next month because her sister had to enter

Stanford University next semester and the whole family was going on home leave. This was the first time I had heard Shirley name a date when they would be leaving, and I instantly felt abandoned and betrayed even as she was sitting next to me. Hot tears stung my eyes and I looked away. "I didn't know you were leaving so soon. You never told me," I said.

Shirley shrugged her shoulders and said, "I forgot. I was going to tell you soon. Honest. Anyway, we still have the whole summer ahead."

The quartet was playing a medley of Russian songs and my mother was deep in animated conversation with Shirley, while I kept poking my spoon into my totally disarrayed, melted sundae, watching the Victoria begin to fill with people and thinking about life without Shirley. Shirley ordered an iced tea, and it was brought to her in a tall glass with a long spoon sticking out of it. It was then that the disaster happened. As the waiter was about to set the glass on the table, Shirley's shoulder got in the way, which caused the glass to fall and spill its contents in her lap. And then, somehow her other hand brushed the plate in front of her, and the remains of the American Sundae landed in her lap too. For a moment no one moved; we just stared at the mess of ice cubes, chocolate cookies, and three shades of ice cream on Shirley's sailor-suit skirt. Then Shirley jumped up and screamed, "I hate the Victoria!" and ran into the bathroom and my mother ran after her while I sat and finished my kuchka and the quartet played "Marche Militaire."

After a while my mother and Shirley returned, looking tired and distant, as if they had come back from a long journey and had now decided that traveling together was not for them. Shirley looked at her Mickey Mouse watch and said she was sure the chauffeur was waiting for her. She didn't sit down but stood by the table and expressed her thanks for a "lovely afternoon" in a clipped manner. She walked over to me and said, "See ya Monday," and walked out of the cafe swinging her bright red purse on its brass chain. For a moment I sat stunned by Shirley's departure—then I got up and ran after her. She was standing by the door waiting for the chauffeur to bring the car around.

"Why are you leaving?" I said.

"I hate the Victoria. I never did want to come here. It's a bore."

"Don't be mad, Shirl. I want us to be friends."

"You're so serious all the time. And so *sensitive*. My mother's always telling me to be careful of your feelings. She says all Jewish people are supersensitive. All I want is to have fun."

I stared at Shirley, thinking this was the first time we had ever discussed my Jewishness. I didn't know how to talk about it.

"I want to have fun, too," I said. "I really do."

"Well, you certainly don't act like it."

The black embassy car drove up and Shirley ran toward it with a swing of her bright red bag. "Ta-ta," she threw over her shoulder.

I walked back into the Victoria. My mother was finishing her sundae and seemed to be really enjoying herself. She was still swaying with the music and nodding to various people.

"Shirley took it quite well—the accident, I mean," said my mother. "Didn't make a fuss."

"She was just being polite. She hated it here."

"Well, there's nothing wrong in being polite."

"I want to go home," I said.

"We will—soon." She looked at me and patted my hand. "And we did return the hospitality. Now you can go to the Canberrys' with a clear conscience."

"I'll probably never get invited again. Besides, they're leaving town soon—you heard Shirley say so."

On Monday morning Shirley and I met outside the schoolyard, where we always waited for each other so we could share the events of the week-end. We had a favorite elm tree that had a bench built around its huge trunk. Shirley was late, and the bell rang just as she was about to sit down, so we had to rush to class. She was sick the next two days, and on Thursday she told me that her parents were having a big embassy party and she couldn't have me over. In the next few weeks she began to see a lot of Marianne Webster, another embassy "kid," and I saw them at the elm tree before the morning bell.

"How's Shirley?" my mother asked.

"She has a new friend."

"Well, we did return the hospitality. You'll probably be friends again," my mother tried to reassure me.

"I don't think so. She never speaks to me now."

My mother hugged me. "I know. It's hard."

I didn't see much of Shirley that summer. In August I got an invitation to her going-away party—a fancy dress party, with music by the Victoria's quartet. I came as a gypsy, and Shirley was dressed up as Marie Antoinette.

"I thought you hated getting dressed up. I thought you only liked camping," I said.

Shirley shrugged her shoulders and cocked her head, her huge white wig tilting to one side. "Well, I've changed my mind. These past few months Marianne and I have been dressing up lots. And I kinda like the quartet. They're cute."

I looked at Mr. Berman dressed in his smoking jacket and tie. He did not look cute to me. He looked tired and uncomfortable. I saw him slap a mosquito and brush off sweat as he bowed his violin.

"I don't think they're cute. They're just trying to make a living . . . and you've changed. You used to hate all this."

Shirley looked at me and sighed. "That's the trouble with you. You're too serious. So I've changed. 'You got to go with the times!' That's what my mother says. Come on, have some fun!"

I hated the party and sat in a corner feeling miserable, watching all the embassy kids dancing and giggling. I decided that my mother was probably right and Shirley would have been uncomfortable in our house with only one bathroom.

I didn't say good-bye to either Shirley or the rest of the Canberrys. I left just as the quartet started playing music to the Virginia Reel and the whole backyard became a whirling kaleidoscope of color. Shirley's brother, Kent, was standing outside their house and he looked bored and asked if I was leaving and I said yes I was and he said "'Bye" and that was all.

Then the war broke out and I never heard from Shirley again.

Figurines, Delicate

I SAT IN the white wicker chair on our veranda in a state of adolescent stupor and irritability waiting for something to happen. We had just moved to a new apartment house on Colombo Road. Bored, bored and boring, I thought to myself. Bored and boring as last year's snow. Bored and boring as leftover gravy. I tried to think of more boring things to amuse myself with, but nothing came. I could hear my mother talking to her friend Vera about the latest gossip in Tientsin, their voices droning on, buzzing like flies in the summer heat. *Plop*! A book fell at my feet, and a voice with a clipped British accent said, "Oh, dear, I dropped my book. Awfully sorry. I'm Mrs. Palmer-Jones, new upstairs neighbor. Could you be a dear and pop up and bring it to me?" Leaping out of my chair like an uncoiled jack-in-the-box, I whizzed by my mother and Vera, yelling, "I'm going upstairs to return a book."

The door to apartment 3 was wide open. "I'm Glenda Palmer-Jones. Call me Glenda." A cigarette dangled from her red lips, and she looked refreshingly cool in a soft blue silk, which hung gracefully on her thin body. "This is Graham," she said, pointing to a towheaded, chunky five-year-old. "Thanks for returning the book. Graham, you must learn to wear shoes. What will our new neighbor think?"

"But she's barefoot," said Graham, pointing to me.

"She's a grown-up, Graham, and can do what she likes."

Never in all my fourteen years had I been referred to as a grown-up, and Glenda's words bathed me in an unfamiliar warm glow. Not bored or boring, I sang to myself. I'm a grown-up. Up-grown. All-grown.

"Come in," said Glenda, waving me into a room, a replica of ours downstairs in size and shape, but there the similarity ended. Books everywhere. On shelves, on the coffee table, books on the floor and unopened crates marked BOOKS. A photo of the royal family standing on the balcony of Windsor Palace, waving to the crowds, stood on a small black mahogany table. Looking closer, I saw that Princess Elizabeth was scowling. Princess Margaret looked bored. How could she possibly be bored, I wondered, with all the things she has at her disposal?

"The royal family. Reminds me of home. We're British," said Glenda, flicking nonexistent dust off the frame with her red-lacquered nails. "And new in Tientsin. Kailan Mining people, actually. Mr. P.J. (that's what I call my husband) is out of town a lot on business, so I'm here alone. Graham and I. If you like books and enjoy some company, you can come up here anytime."

I knew Kailan Mining Company—coal was their business. Their main offices were housed in a gigantic gray building next to the park. Two Sikh guards patrolled it day and night. Utterly ferocious-looking in their turbanned headgear, they had frightened me as a child, and to this day I crossed the street in order to avoid them.

"You can borrow any book you want to. What do you like? Short stories? Poetry? Translations of Chinese poems?"

"Somerset Maugham and Chekhov," I said.

"Good choices. But how about some poems by Li Fa?"

Glenda looked straight at me, her eyes transparent like a cat's. I felt pinned down, as if I were a mouse under a soft, heavy paw. I squirmed, feeling embarrassed.

"I don't know Li Fa."

"My dear, I can't believe you are living in China and don't know Li Fa. He is a very important thirteenth-century poet. You must read him. You absolutely must. How long have you lived here?"

"I was born here. But my parents came from Russia," I added, as if to justify my ignorance about Chinese literature.

"Gracious. We must correct your ignorance. Mr. P.J. and I have been in

China since last December. We were first stationed in Peking, and we will
be here for another two years. We have promised ourselves, Mr. P.J. and I,
that we will learn everything we can while we are here. You do realize that
the way to a country's soul is through its literature."

I came away with a book of stories by Maugham and a slim volume of
poetry by Li Fa. Later that evening I told my mother that Glenda had invited me to come upstairs and borrow books as often as I wanted to. My
mother said it was a great idea and now I wouldn't have to go all the way
downtown to the library. She reminded me to limit my time upstairs and
not become a nuisance. My father thought it would be good practice for
me to hear a cultured British voice.

After a few weeks, Glenda suggested I come up regularly. "Tuesdays
would be a good time. We can chat, have tea, and we can talk about the
books you read. We'll exchange ideas."

My parents were astonished at the routine. "I can see why you like it up
there—a whole library for you. But what on earth does she get out of talking to a child?" said my mother. My father felt that Mrs. P.J. was desperately lonely and needed a companion. Both reminded me not to be a
bother and to be polite. By the end of summer I couldn't remember a time
when I had not gone upstairs on Tuesdays.

Glenda always sat on the sofa with her bare feet curled under her, in some
shimmering dress that flowed and billowed, tentlike, around her body when
she got up. When she rang a silver bell, Liu the houseboy appeared and
brought tea and cucumber sandwiches. Sometimes he brought hard biscuits
with scalloped edges that had "Bristol" stamped on them. Graham usually
sat on the floor playing with his toy trains or leafing through picture books.

When reading, Glenda kept her head close to the page, and her bangs
covered her face. But when she looked up I was always startled by her eyes,
which seemed to sizzle and burn, like pale blue diamonds. Her conversations were incandescent and intense, and sometimes I wondered if she was
sick with a fever.

"Have you been to the Chinese part of the city recently?" she whispered
hoarsely one day as she leaned toward me, cupping her head in her blue-
veined palm.

"No. I'm not allowed to go there."

"Why?"

On a rare visit to the Chinese part of Tientsin.

"Mother says it's dangerous. Too many thieves. And dirty. We usually do not go out of the concessions."

Glenda stared at me unblinkingly. Finally she leaned across a pile of books, thrust her face close to mine, and said, "You mean you *never* go there? Is that what you mean?"

I admitted shamefacedly that it was true. I had been allowed to go to the Chinese part of the city once, but that was many years ago, and the memory had already faded.

"No matter. You and I, we must go. Together. And we'll take Graham with us. Graham and I have been there before. Oh, the sights and sounds of China. The charming little alleys filled with all sorts of barbaric smells." Glenda wrinkled her nose and clapped her hands. "The fish sold live in the tanks. And the children running around with slits in their pants, doing you-know-what right on the streets. Not very sanitary, my dear, but economical. I am writing it all down in my diary. We must go someday, the three of us. I shall ask Mr. P.J. to get the chauffeur to drive us."

Sweeping Graham off the floor, she danced around with him in her

arms. Graham roared with laughter. Glenda chirped like a bright little bird
and sang, "A-merrily we will go, a-merrily we will go."

When I told my parents about the proposed trip, my father said, "Naive
foreigners, these British and Americans. They think it is so quaint here.
They should live here for real. Then they would change their minds and
see what it is really like." My mother said, "I think you should stop going
upstairs. That Englishwoman is filling your head with all sorts of strange
thoughts and ideas."

One rainy afternoon I brought a short story for Glenda to read. She
read it out loud, and I became so dizzy with joy at hearing my writing for
the first time that I felt as if a large bird was expanding its wings against
my rib cage, leaving no room for the air to flow through. "You're quite
good, my dear," said Glenda with a smile. "Quite good. You need to work,
but you have potential."

Every Tuesday I climbed the stairs to Glenda's apartment, my mind at
odds with itself. As if twin souls walked up, one excited about seeing
Glenda, the other wary of what lay ahead. Discomfort and joy flowed side
by side in my cage.

One day while we were reading and the room was quiet except for an
occasional grunt from Graham, Glenda's foot started tapping nervously
and little puffs of dust rose from the chair.

"How many servants do you have?" she asked. I had grown used to her
startling questions that seemed to spring from some deep river inside her
and float like bright, astonishing packages to the surface.

"Two." I waited apprehensively for her to continue.

"Do you know their families?" Glenda was creeping toward me on the
couch, her eyes blazing, her lips slightly parted. I could see her perfectly
formed alabaster teeth. A thought floated in my head. If she had whiskers,
Glenda would look like a cat. I felt a shiver of anticipation. Fear.

"No, I don't know their families."

"You should, my dear. You really should get to know them. Their
hopes. Their fears. Their hearts. Do you realize you are living in a bell jar
here? Around you are the riches of a most exotic culture and you sit blind
to it. We must do something about that. Otherwise you'll end up being
the worst kind of colonial there is. A total uncaring prig."

"I don't want to do anything about it," I said, suddenly feeling sullen and heavy. "And I'm not a colonial. You are. All I want to do is to read books."

"My dear. We are both colonials. As to reading, the purpose of that is to enlarge your horizons. To educate. To better yourself and to expand. I just want to help you achieve that."

"I don't want to expand. This is my summer break. I just want to read books."

Glenda arched her back, stretched her hands out in front of her, and said to Graham, "Now, Graham, we are going to have to do all those wonderful things by ourselves. Our girl from downstairs doesn't want to join us. We'll go and then we'll tell her about our adventures. Won't we, Gramikins?"

"Yes, Mumsie, we will," said Graham as he threw himself into her lap. She started stroking his flaxen hair, and they continued purring and stroking each other, Glenda's brilliant blue dress encircling Graham's head, their arms around each other. I said good-bye, but they didn't hear me as I tiptoed out.

I dreamt that night that I was a mouse, living next door to an elegant, sleek cat who stared at me all day long. I wanted to play with the cat, but every time I got near her she would whip out her paw and try to squash me. I noticed, however, that the paws had no claws, so I inched toward this magnificent creature, trying to get close. Then the paw came down gently on my head. I could feel its soft calluses. Soon I was close to the cat's body, sitting underneath the stomach. I could hear purrs that sounded like thunder. Still, I was not scared. I was elated. But then the cat began to put all her weight on me, squashing me with her body, taking my breath away. I was suffocating and awoke unable to breathe.

Tuesday came and went. I was in town when I realized what day it was, and it gave me a certain amount of pleasure to know I had stood Glenda up. Briefly I told my friend Mira about her. Mira said, "You should stick with your own kind. What on earth do you have in common with an older Englishwoman? The English—they're so stuck up, think the sun never sets on anything British." I said Glenda wasn't stuck up but that she was different. "How different?" pushed Mira. "Well, she treats me like a grown-up, asks questions." "Well, I ask questions." "That's not the same," I said, feeling irritated and changing the subject.

When I got home there was a note from Glenda. "Graham and I miss our girl from downstairs. Have a new tin of biscuits and two new crates of books just arrived from London."

I flew upstairs and knocked on the door. Glenda's cheery voice answered, and she welcomed me, not mentioning the note or my absence. She motioned me to the sofa and pointed to the new tin of biscuits on the coffee table.

"Graham and I have started Chinese lessons. Graham is doing wonderfully, but I'm having difficulties. The shifts in sound are so delicate, and yet the entire meaning changes completely with each little nuance. Have you found it so?"

"I speak very little Chinese."

Glenda raised her eyebrows. "Really! It's such a rich language. You don't speak it? Why?"

"There is no need," said I, feeling my teeth clenching.

"No need!"

"Yes, no need," I said guardedly, withholding each word as Glenda chattered persistently. How was I ever to explain this feeling of wrongness I had about living in China, a feeling so tiresome that I always fell asleep before I could sort it out?

"Well, my dear. How do you speak to the servants?" Glenda's voice was cheerful, ignoring my reserve.

"English. They know English. Or Russian."

"You are acting just like all colonials. Imposing your will and your language on the natives. You mustn't do that. You really ought not to,"

I looked at Glenda, who was leaning against the back of the sofa with her eyes closed. She looked tired.

"You ask too many questions, Glenda," I blurted out, feeling immediately shaky at my sudden ferocity. "I don't know how to answer you."

Glenda remained quiet, her eyes still shut, and I wondered if I had hurt her and now could never come upstairs again. She sighed, did not answer, picked up a book and began reading. I picked up the nearest book, which was Scott Fitzgerald, and was soon swept away into Daisy's flirtatious world.

Glenda rang for tea, and after sipping a few drops, she threw a ravishing smile in my direction and said, "I have a treat for you. I'm going to

read some poetry out loud. Graham loves it. It's the poetry of Shie Yuan."
She picked up a slim, battered volume, uncurled her feet, put her hands
in her lap like an obedient little schoolgirl, opened the book, and began
reading. Leaning back against the soft velvet sofa pillows, I resigned myself to this ordeal. To my amazement, I found Glenda's bell-like voice
soothing. She read slowly and intensely, savoring each word.

"Well, that wasn't too bad, was it?" Glenda said with a laugh.

"Actually, I liked it."

"See, new things can be expanding. Seeing things in the old way is
being a stick-in-the-mud."

Graham jumped up and started yelling, "Stick-in-the-mud, stick-in-
the-mud," and Glenda joined him as they both sang, "Stick-in-the-mud."

"How about taking these poems home with you?" said Glenda with a
twinkle in her eye as she thrust the book into my hands.

"No, thanks. I like when you read them, but I really prefer short stories."

For a moment Glenda held the book in her outstretched hand, as if not
knowing what to do with it, and we stared at each other like two pugilists
before the bell goes off. Then she put the book on the table and walked
over to the glassed-in china cabinet where she kept her collection of Chinese porcelain figurines. She took out a little cloth and began polishing
them. Her back was to me. "See you next week," she said, throwing the
words over her shoulder. She held up one little figure against the light,
then she laid it against her cheek, rubbing it slowly against the skin. She
did not turn around when I left the room.

School started in late September and I was busy Tuesdays. I thought of
going upstairs and telling Glenda about my new schedule, but somehow
it didn't seem right. Once I ran into her in the foyer. She and Graham
were rosy-cheeked and dressed in riding clothes. "We've been pony riding
at the country club, Mommy and me," said Graham. Glenda smiled politely and said, "We must get together soon," but there was no weight to
her words. They slipped away from her lips like drops of spilled tea. We
made plans that day for the return of several books of short stories that I
still had in my possession.

In October winter had made its first imprint on the city, spilling flurries of early snow on the rooftops. One morning I saw movers come into

the upstairs apartment and carry out a lot of furniture. Graham was playing hopscotch by himself in the garden, and I questioned him.

"Mummy's sister Alice died and we have to go home," he said.

I was shocked to find that Glenda had a sister. She had never talked about her family, and I had never asked her about her life in England. We had always focused on me. I was filled with a sense of disquiet, a feeling of disorder that I could not identify. Glenda came into the garden, her eyes red from crying, her hair hastily combed and tied at the nape of her neck with a red string.

"Wouldn't you know," she said, addressing her words to no one in particular, "I have all this packing to do and it is Liu's day off and Mr. P.J. is out of town. I called the embassy and they said they'd send a man to help pack, but he's not here, so Graham and I are packing ourselves."

"I'll help," I offered. "You should have asked me. I would have been glad to do it."

"Well, yes, I suppose. But I probably should have asked your parents and we . . . well, we never really got acquainted."

I went upstairs with Glenda. The room was empty except for several crates marked BOOKS and one marked FIGURINES, DELICATE. A shudder ran down my spine. It was like seeing death.

"I didn't know you had a sister," I said.

"Gwen. She's been sickly for years. Had polio as a child and then last month caught pneumonia. Mother telegraphed and wanted me and Graham to come for the funeral."

"I'm sorry we never talked about your family," I said.

"You never asked." Glenda's eyes were downcast, and I thought I detected a touch of irony but wasn't sure.

She asked me to help her with a crate. I knelt down beside her and held one side of the crate while she slipped a heavy rope underneath, tying the ends neatly in a bow on top.

"Sometimes I've thought I asked you too many questions. And in my usual pell-mell sort of way. Mr. P.J. always says I probe too much. Tells me I should be more reserved, not so impatient and wait for opportunities. But I'm Welsh, you know. Not British. We're very emotional. I hope I didn't upset you. I really was curious. I'm a teacher at heart."

Before I had time to respond, Graham ran up the stairs yelling, "The embassy person is here, and he says we must go immediately." When Glenda stood in the middle of the empty room, motionless, Graham rushed up to her, tugged at her hand, and said, "Now, Mummy. We have to go now."

"In a minute, Graham," said Glenda in a quiet voice. She stretched out her hands, spreading her fingers wide and slowly pirouetted around the room.

"I loved being in China. So much to learn. I will never forget this remarkable experience. Or you," she said turning to me. She picked up the only book still uncrated and gave it to me. It was the slim volume of poems by Li Fa.

"Someday you might like it."

I took it without saying a word. I heard the car starting and Graham shouting, "Yippee, we're going on a trip." Glenda flew down the stairs into the waiting car, the embassy man standing at attention until she sank into the seat, then smartly closing the door.

Later that evening, I sat in my room and opened the book of poems. For an hour I read, and before going to bed I looked out and saw the Chinese beggar on the street corner. It was a familiar sight. He always slept there under his rags, huddled into a tight ball. Tomorrow I will speak to him, I thought. Tomorrow I will ask his name.

December 8, 1941

I WAKE UP to small flurries of snow patches plopping against my second-floor window. The early-morning December light, anemic and sickly, does not rouse in me any desire to get up. Snuggling deeper into my peacock silk quilt, I wish I could lie here forever, burrowed into my soft nest, hibernating like a fuzzy bear, and not go to school. But a big snowflake sizzles on the windowpane, hissing urgent messages. "Get up, get up."

Cautiously putting my feet on the cold floor, I drag myself to the window to make my acquaintance with the day. Across the street is the British Embassy, a gloomy, sprawling mansion. I look for the red, white, and blue Union Jack that swings from a pole in the middle of the compound. Every day I greet it from my window. On windy days the flag writhes, catching the dancing air, its stripes bunched up and tangled. In light breezes it billows; in rain it hangs limply; in the summer it is a brazen, glorious flag, spread out like a soaring eagle. But today it is nowhere to be found. I search for it as for a favored companion, anxiety creeping up to my temples, a heavy feeling of loss swirling in my stomach.

It has disappeared. Maybe they moved it. Maybe a new and grander spot has been found for it. Through the spattered, icy window I desperately mount my search. I have never gone to school without greeting the flag.

My eyes try to pierce the icy air and sweep to all four corners of the embassy compound. A barren emptiness encircles the grounds. No dogs are

taking their morning walk. No servants are bustling around. No garden-
ers. The muscular, turbanned Sikhs who usually guard the front gate are
not there. The massive gates, always closed, now stand open, flapping
wearily on their hinges. There are no automobiles entering or leaving. The
regal mansion seems to have sunk under the weight of a snow blanket like
a tired dowager, waiting for something.

I feel a hushed nervousness in the air, muffled by the falling snow.
Undefinable evil sits moodily on treetops. Tension bruises the leaves.
Nothing moves.

Surely tomorrow will return to normal.

It is December 8, 1941.

11. *Occupation*

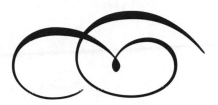

Men Talking

FIRST MAN: I tell you, gentlemen, let's go with the Portuguese offer. They're offering us papers, for heaven's sake, let's take them! Our current I.D.'s are useless. Do we have a consensus?

FATHER: But we will anger the Japanese. If we remain uncommitted the Japanese will think we're on their side.

FIRST MAN: That's the whole trouble with us Jews. Trying to figure out what the other folks want. Trying to please them. I say we'll be better off with real passports. The Japanese will respect us more.

FATHER: But it will cost. Quite a bit. I hear the Portuguese want at least 80,000 yuan for each passport.

FIRST MAN: So is anything free? Of course it costs. But we'll have proper documents, not dinky cards that say "stateless."

SECOND MAN: I think we should consult Hanin.

FIRST MAN: Hanin, Shmanin. He isn't here. Can't we think for ourselves?

FATHER: Hanin should be talked to. He knows where the current wind blows. He knows how to smell things out.

FIRST MAN: The wind tells me, gentlemen, that there is a big stink, a regular cesspool coming if we don't take action.

Our stateless passports during the war. Left, my father's, and below, my mother's and mine.

SECOND MAN: I hear Gurevich already has bought himself a Portuguese passport. Calls himself Gurevich Pereira.

(laughs)

THIRD MAN: I say "a rose is a rose" and "a Jew is a Jew" whatever he has. No one will ever think that Gurevich is Portuguese.

FIRST MAN: Gentlemen, gentlemen. No one is trying to fool anyone. All I'm saying is that we need proper documents. Proper papers. The Portuguese Embassy, at a price, is offering us citizenship and protection. Now, can't we agree on that?

SECOND MAN: I still think we need to talk to Hanin. Let's wait till our next meeting.

FIRST MAN: (out of control) I've had it! I'm resigning! Talk, talk, and more talk!

FATHER: Now, now, things will work out.

The Japanese Soldiers
Who Came in the Night

WE SHARED TSUI, our new cook, who performed miracles with rotting vegetables and worm-ridden flour, as well as keeping the parquet floors
smartly polished and the brass doorknobs so shiny that you could see your
face reflected in them if you stooped low enough. We also shared the flat
at 12 rue St. Louis. The Fleishmans and we were doubled up in a space
large enough for one family but snug for two, because the Japanese had occupied China and housing was scarce in Tientsin in the winter of 1941.
Coal was even scarcer, and we shared the puny dung-spattered pellets,
which Tsui kept in an enormous metal coal bin by the stove. The American School had closed, and I, together with the Fleishman girls, went to
the Tientsin Jewish School.

At the end of each month my mother and Mrs. Fleishman sat down at
our dining room table, pushed the lace tablecloth to one side, had Tsui
bring in a pot of tea, and did their accounts. "Coal, twenty thousand
yuan." "I spent three thousand yuan on flour last week, even though it had
two capfuls of worms." "Honey was on sale yesterday, so I stocked up on
it." Their voices droned on. At the end of this monthly ritual, they would
call Tsui in and give him his salary.

I liked Tsui and admired his agile way of closing doors with one flip of
his foot while balancing a tray in his hands. He was tall and totally bald.
He was also our expert on window taping. We had been ordered by the

Japanese occupation forces to have our windows taped and our curtains light-proofed to guard against possible American air raids. Tsui often let me help him cut the newspaper strips, dip them into a murky mixture of flour and water and then crisscross the panes with them. The trick was not to let the long strips stick to each other or dry out, which would render them totally useless. This took dexterity. I had none, but Tsui was patient with me.

I often dreamt of being bombed, imagining high window-glass shards dangling like icicles on the tape and the wind whistling through the broken glass. One day I dreamt that lush tropical fruits—pineapples, bananas, and kumquats—hung on the strips. Every morning I checked to see if the strips were still in place.

"You shouldn't be following Tsui around," my mother would say. "He has his work to do and you have yours. And stop going downstairs. Your place is here—upstairs."

It mystified me, this talk of "place." Why was Tsui always upstairs in my place, and I could never go to his? "That's the way things are," I was told by my parents in a kindly, throwaway fashion that made trite and commonplace what was obviously serious and controversial. My mother would wrinkle her nose, and my father would close his eyes, which signaled the end of the conversation.

One evening I heard the Fleishmans getting ready for their evening walk, arguing loudly about the route to take. "We shall go on the Bund all the way to Victoria Park, and that's final!" I heard Mr. Fleishman's growl, followed by silence and the patter of feet as the family, single file, trooped out. Tsui came in to clear the dinner dishes and fold the card table. We ate in the bedroom, which was the only heated room in our part of the flat. Everything we needed for the winter months was in this room, including the grand piano, which worried my mother because it stood so close to the potbellied stove. "It will ruin the tone," she would often ruminate.

After dinner I began practicing Chopin's "Minute Waltz," racing to see how fast I could go. Recently, I had been able to do it in under three minutes. I fantasized about the look of pleasure on my piano teacher's face at my next lesson. After getting totally out of breath from the waltz, I switched to the first movement of the "Pathetique," its ponderous notes falling like heavy snow on the sizzling red-hot coal pellets. Wind gusts beat against the windowpanes. Tsui came in to check the black-velvet curtains for light leaks. With a safety pin, he closed a gap and left the room.

Suddenly there was a knock on the front door. I froze my fingers in mid-bar. My foot fell heavily on the pedal, and the room reverberated with the D minor chord.

"Take your foot off the pedal," my father hissed with fear.

"Wonder who it could be," said my mother, looking up from her knitting. The knocking persisted. Someone was pounding furiously and screaming harsh, guttural Japanese words. My mother's needles made a *clackety-clack* sound. Faster and faster they went. My father casually picked up a newspaper and began reading it. I noticed it was upside down.

"Should we open the door?" said my father, his voice studiously calm. "It's probably the Japanese sentry on patrol to check our windows. But you know what an expert Tsui is, everything is no doubt shipshape. No need to worry."

"Maybe the sentry is cold and wants to come and warm himself," my mother said hopefully.

"Maybe we should be quiet and pretend no one is at home. Last week a sentry came to the Golmans' door and complained that their curtains leaked light. They had to appear the next day at the police station and spent hours waiting for someone to speak to them."

"Did they take away their ration cards?" I said. That was the worst disaster I could think of.

"No. But they certainly intimidated them. Never can tell when they'll pick on something to harass you with. Mrs. Golman was afraid to go out for days. Sometimes people never come back from those interviews. Never."

My parents both sighed and their eyes hooded over, as if they were looking at something I could not see. They were frozen in a landscape that I did not understand.

"Is that how Willie's father disappeared? After an interview at the police station?"

"How do you know that?"

"The kids talk about it at school. And I've seen Willie crying during recess."

"Don't think about it. Forget it. The less you know, the better, nowa-days. Just pay attention to your studies."

The pounding was now a crescendo of noise. I could hear the sound of metal against our wooden front door. Someone was pulling at the doorknob as if to extract it like an inflamed tooth from its socket. The doorknobs were Tsui's pride and joy, and I wondered how he would feel about this assault on his property.

"We're going to have to let them in. They're not going to go away."

"Play something," my mother whispered. "Let's just make it look like an ordinary evening."

"What shall I play?" I asked.

"Anything. Anything. Well, how about Schubert's 'Impromptu'? That should soothe them."

"They don't know anything about European music. It's a foolish idea." My father's voice squeaked with tension.

But my mother insisted and ordered me to play.

"Keep playing while we go to the front door."

I started the "Impromptu." From the scraping of chairs behind me, I knew that my parents were leaving the room. I looked straight ahead, my fingers automatically striking the keys. My hands felt puffy and swollen, as if bitten by some insect, and there was a ringing in my left ear, the one that had been operated on for mastoids. I wanted to jump up and follow my parents. I wanted to tell them not to go to the police station, and I wanted to tell them to come back and never go for any interviews. By now I was in the second movement of the "Impromptu." My parents had still not returned. The tears welled up in my throat, settling there in a briny, choking mass.

Bang! Crash! The front door was flung open. Two harsh voices and the sound of boots crunching on the parquet floors. My God, I thought to myself, there are two of them—not one. My parents' voices were low, con-ciliatory, but they were there. They had not disappeared. Relief coursed through me.

Finally, the door to our room was flung open, and two Japanese soldiers stood in front of me, with my parents standing meekly behind them. My father smiled wanly at me and shrugged his shoulders, as if to say, This will be over soon. The soldiers swayed back and forth on the heels of their fur-lined boots, holding their rifles in front of them. Then they both walked over to the stove and started warming their hands, taking off their grubby leather gloves and spreading their fingers wide to catch the heat.

"I told you so. They're just cold," said my mother in a reassuring voice.

"And so young," chimed in my father.

"Maybe we should offer them some tea," said my mother, but no one moved. We stood around the stove awkwardly.

The taller soldier moved away from the stove first and walked up to the windows. He inspected the curtains carefully for holes and frayed cloth. He strutted back and forth as if on a parade ground. March. March. No words were uttered. I was standing by the piano and my hand accidentally fell on the piano keys. The noise slit the quiet like the squeal of a slaughtered pig. The soldier stopped. He jabbed a finger toward the ceiling and uttered some loud, guttural sound. He kept jabbing and screaming, and finally we realized that he wanted to inspect the upper part of the windows—too high for him to reach. He was going to be thorough. My father hastily brought him a chair and the soldier smartly jumped on it. He began to poke the velvet curtains with his rifle. He then unhooked the safety pins that held the curtains together and began examining the tapes on the window. I held my breath, for I realized as soon as he opened the curtains that several of the strips had dried out and were hanging loosely on the glass. He saw that too, for he jumped off the chair, rushed over to my father, grabbed him by his shirt, and pushed him toward the offending window. Pressing my father's face close to the glass, he pointed at the dried tape with his rifle and pulled off a strip, throwing it on the ground.

He spat out a torrent of incomprehensible sounds and pushed my father away from him. In his hand he held a piece of my father's shirt. He stared at it for a while, held it between his thumb and forefinger like a poisonous snake, and then threw it angrily into the red-hot stove. The pellets sizzled and burst into flames. I held my breath, feeling its gathering force almost exploding in my chest. I glanced at the soldier, who was now staring at his shoes, his body limp as if exhausted. The room was quiet and we waited, not knowing for what. He raised his head and looked at us, huddling together like a pack of shivering animals. This sight seemed to enrage him, and he started his tirade all over again. Words spilled out of his mouth with such intensity that saliva dribbled down, leaving little spots on the dusty buttons of his collar.

The second soldier had been standing all this time by the stove, poking the fire with the long, slender poker and not paying any attention to his companion, who was obviously the one in charge. He seemed quite cheerful, enjoying the warm fire on his outstretched hands. He wiggled his fingers and smiled. There was something familiar about him, and as he looked up at me and took off his visored cap, I realized I had seen him before.

Last week I had gone walking in the park. The mimosa and birch trees were barren, their branches a dark filigree of black against the gray November sky. I was bored and restless and was about to return home when I heard a child's cry. Not far from me, in a swing, I saw a heavily bundled child who was trying futilely to push herself. Although I had been warned not to play with the "occupation army's children," I decided to swing the child anyway. I knew I was about to disobey a rule, but a minute flame of rebellion had recently been brewing in me. I also knew well the feeling of utter frustration when one is ground-stuck in a swing. I walked over to the child, stood behind her, and gave her a push. She giggled with delight. The harder I pushed, the more she giggled. Then I got into the swing next to her and we both shrieked with total delight and abandon as our swings went higher and higher. Beyond the trees we swung. Over the houses. Straight into the gray sky we pushed.

A man came up and watched us. He and the child exchanged words. We kept swinging, now both on our feet, bending our knees to get more leverage on the board. The ropes were chafing my palms. The man watched quietly. When we finally stopped, the child ran to the man, who I assumed was her father, and put her hand in his. He took out a pair of mittens and put them on her hands. We stood around awkwardly, as if waiting for something to happen. I spoke no Japanese. They obviously spoke no English. The man took off his cap and held it in his hands in front of him. Suddenly, I remembered I had my Brownie with me. I brought it out for the child and the man. They smiled and without any direction from me began to pose. First they sat down on a bench side by side. Then they stood up. Finally, the man sat on the bench and the child stood behind him. This seemed to satisfy him. Neither smiled. I clicked the camera, and then they broke into broad smiles. "Thank you," I said. They both bowed and left.

When the pictures were developed, my parents reminded me that I had been told not to play with Japanese children. "Who knows what could happen? And taking their pictures! They could hold it against us," said my father.

"How could they do that?"

This irritated my father. "They could say you were trying to get too friendly."

"What's wrong with that?"

"That it could lead to your requesting special favors from them."

"What's wrong with that?" I knew I was pushing my father, but I just couldn't understand how taking a picture of the child and her father would harm me.

"They are the occupation. We are the occupied. We are not supposed to fraternize. Mingle. That's the way things are."

I had hidden the photo in my drawer, under my pajamas, although I had been told to destroy it. The soldier by the stove was now smiling at me. It was a little smile, as if he was hiding it from his companion, who was still marching up and down examining things, growling. I rushed over to my drawer, took out the picture, looked at my parents defiantly, and thrust it into his hands.

The soldier looked at the picture and grinned. He pointed at the picture, then at me, and laughed, a full belly laugh, a not-holding-back laugh. He went over to his companion and showed him the picture. The companion stared at it with angry eyes. He was not amused. He and the soldier exchanged words, harsh accusatory sounds, and then he looked away and continued his pacing up and down the room.

My parents by now were sitting down. They looked exhausted and old. I wanted my father to say something, anything, but he sat with closed eyes, holding the tear in his shirt with one hand, kneading the material as if to make it whole again.

The soldier kept admiring the picture. Then he began searching in his pocket for something. He took out a worn wallet, looked through its contents, and finally brought out a faded newspaper clipping. He handed it to me. I could barely make out the faces. It looked like a family. Parents and two children stared sternly at me from the photograph. Judging from the attire, they were a well-to-do family. I handed the clipping to my father.

"I think it is the emperor and his family. Too faded to really tell. Probably a clipping from a Japanese newspaper."

I handed the clipping back to the soldier, but he pushed my hand back and refused to take it.

"I think he wants to give it to you. To keep. Because you gave him the picture you took."

"Do you think I ought to? What about not fraternizing and all that?" I said, and I realized I was standing up to my father, challenging him. It felt good but also a little sad.

"I know I said that. But in this case . . . I think you're going to have to take the picture. Otherwise he will be offended."

I looked at the soldier. He was beaming at me. I took the clipping and put it in my drawer.

"Sank you, sank you," he said, pointing to the photo I had given him.

I tried to think of a Japanese phrase to say in return. All I could think of was "*sodes-ne*" (that is so), one of the few phrases I knew. We kept repeating these words to each other. He bowed. I bowed.

The companion, who was obviously getting tired of all this friendliness, whispered something to the soldier. They exchanged words. Suddenly, my friend (I was beginning to think of him as a friend) looked at me sternly and stiffened his body. He dropped the poker on the hearth. He put on his gloves. He pressed his cap tight on his skull and yanked at the visor. He barked some words at my parents, swung abruptly on his heel, and swept out of the room, followed by his companion. Their boots clomped heavily in the hallway. *Clomp. Clomp.* All the way to the front door, which they slammed with such force that it rattled the teacups on the shelf.

My mother said, "Well. I'm glad that's over." She got up slowly from her chair, as if doing it for the first time, hanging on to the armrests. My father sat crumpled in his chair for several minutes. He got up slowly and went to the window. He was still holding the rent in his shirt. His shoulders were going up and down like slow pistons. Was he crying? Sighing?

Tsui appeared, as if nothing had happened. He cleared the remaining dinner dishes. My father turned from the window and said he was going for a walk to clear his head. I asked to join him.

"You should be in bed," he started to say and then changed his mind and said, "Well, you did save the day, so come along. Who knows what would have happened if the soldier and you had not met in the park? Who knows?"

I felt heavy with pride as we walked out together into the hallway and heard the voices of the Fleishman family returning home.

"Someday this will all end," my father said, giving me a hug as he helped me wind the thick red muffler around my neck. We got into the lift, pressing the down button. The ornate cage slid effortlessly to its destination.

Sammy

"WHY DO YOU always wear your mittens on a string?" Sammy was a year older than me, and his tone was mocking. He picked up one of the mittens, pulled the string it was attached to, and wrapped it around my neck. I looked up into the deep black eyes beneath the bushy eyebrows.

"Because my mother says I will lose them otherwise," I said. Sammy let go of the string and laughed, throwing his head way back. He was leaning against the rickety fence of the Tientsin Jewish School, and it shuddered against his weight.

"Are you always going to do what your mother says? I bet even after the war is over, you'll still be wearing mittens on a string. You'll be wearing your silly mittens, listening to your mother, while I'll be fighting in Palestine for our new state. You just wait and see. I'm going to get out of this crazy place, and no one will stop me."

Sammy was always talking about running away to Palestine. "How in the world are you going to get out of here? There is a war on, you know. And we're occupied by the Japanese, remember?"

Sammy looked mysteriously at me and said, "I'll find a way, you'll see."

"Stop your crazy talk," I said.

"It's not crazy. This place is crazy. I'm going to get out."

"How?"

Sammy looked around the schoolyard, bent his head down toward me,

My Tientsin Jewish School certificate.

and whispered. "First I'm going to go to Shanghai, then to Italy, and then the underground will smuggle me to Palestine."

"What do they want with a fifteen-year-old, Sammy?"

"They need us. To fight the war. To have a state for the Jews. You're just a silly girl and don't understand anything."

We stood glaring at each other. Students were milling around in the narrow schoolyard. It was a cold November day—the beginning of the long Chinese winter—and everyone was bundled up in earmuffs and thick mittens. Sammy was dressed, as usual, in an open-neck brown shirt with a scarf hung casually around his neck, as if defying the very elements. He never even gets cold, I thought to myself. Why can't he be like everyone else? Out of the corner of one eye I saw Bozie pulling Naomi's long, fat braids. Naomi was plump and flirtatious. I could hear her squealing with delight as Bozie tugged her hair. Next to her, Mira and Lily, the school fashion plates, stood quietly waiting for the first bell of the day. Their matching fur coats glistened in the weak morning sun rays, and they wore smart caracul hats with mink brims. Show-offs, I thought to myself. They were looking at Sammy, and I could see his body tighten. He brushed back his hair, patted me casually on the shoulder, took a deep breath, and sauntered toward the girls. I could hear their peals of laughter as he approached.

I hate this place, I thought. I hate China. It's boring, bleak, and nothing will ever happen to me. Why did my parents flee here from Russia? This war is going to go on forever, and I will be stuck here. And Sammy will go and leave me behind.

I watched him as he flirted with Lily and Mira. He took off his scarf, swinging it above his head like a lariat, and I could hear the girls squeal, "Aren't you cold, Sammy? How can you walk around without a jacket?" Sammy strutted in front of them. Why can't he be ordinary? I thought. Once I had heard his mother ask that of my mother. And my mother said it was because of his involvement with the Zionist youth group and the influence of the group's leader, Mr. Barchensky. And Sammy's mother had stared at my mother for the longest time and in a hoarse, guttural voice had said, "That Barchensky, he should have sons. Then he wouldn't be putting all those ideas of going to war and running away to Palestine into Sammy's head. He's a monster, that Barchensky."

The school bell rang. I rushed toward the low brick building where we had our weekly assembly and was soon swallowed up by a group of classmates rushing toward the same place. I looked back. Sammy was still talking to Lily and Mira. "You'll be late," I yelled. He turned around and stared at me. He's mad at me, I thought. Why do I always make him mad? "Come on," I said. "Faster. You know how Mr. Nizer gets mad when we're late, especially when Mr. Fujimoto comes to inspect." Sammy began to move toward the building, and as he passed me he hissed, "Baby, baby. Always following orders."

Everyone was rushing to their assigned spot in the assembly room. The youngsters through form five were in front. Sammy and I were in the back, in the last two rows. Mira and Lily managed to sit on either side of Sammy and I heard their giggles and laughter. Mr. Nizer was anxiously pacing up and down the aisles. "Quiet down, children," he kept pleading. "Quiet down and be sure to do what Mr. Fujimoto tells you to. Please."

The hum in the room subsided as Mr. Fujimoto strutted to the stage at the front of the room. His job was to inspect our school, the Tientsin Jewish School, on a regular basis, and once a month he arrived in a black

limousine, met by Mr. Borotkin, the principal, and Mr. Nizer. It was up
to him to sanction the continued running of our school and to instill in
us a sense of allegiance to the emperor and to Japan. From the loud, guttural sounds that used to come from Mr. Borotkin's office on these
monthly occasions, I felt that our very existence hung on a thread.

Mr. Fujimoto was a small, taut man, always dressed in khaki. He wore
his green-visored cap low on his forehead and carried a nightstick, which
he kept beating against his leg. I heard its rhythmic *swoosh* as he strode toward the stage, followed by Mr. Borotkin with head bowed and hands
clasped behind his back. I looked back at Sammy. He had one arm around
Lily's shoulder and the other around Mira. The girls were grinning.
Sammy winked at me. I quickly turned and stared ahead.

Mr. Fujimoto was now on the stage—pacing back and forth and not
saying a word. Mr. Borotkin sat quietly at the table, his head resting on
his cupped hands. Mr. Nizer had stopped pacing and was leaning against
the wall. Back and forth strode Mr. Fujimoto, slapping his nightstick
against his leg. Abruptly he stopped in the middle of the stage and stared
at the assembly. Then, with a sudden jerk, like a marionette pulled by an
unseen hand, he swung his body round, faced east, thrust both hands upward, fingers spread out wide, and screamed, "BONSAI! BONSAI!" The entire student body leapt to their feet at this cue, thrusting their hands upward, rotating abruptly eastward, and yelling, "BONSAI! BONSAI!" The little
ones in front yelled with great fervor, their childish voices loud and clear.
The enthusiasm of the middle forms was sluggish, and Mr. Nizer hissed
at them, "Louder, louder."

In the last two rows, we too jumped up, but at Sammy's cue. He
shouted, "Down," and we squatted low in the rows. Sammy yelled, "JERU-
SALEM! JERUSALEM!" and we followed, screaming, "JERUSALEM! JERUSA-
LEM!" I held Naomi's hand and we giggled hysterically. Her sharp nails
dug into my palms. Behind me I heard Sammy shout, "Next year in
Jerusalem!" and we chanted "Next year in Jerusalem." Our chants blended
with the "BONSAI! BONSAI!" chant in the front rows. Mr. Nizer rushed toward Sammy and hissed through clenched teeth, "Follow orders, or you'll
get us in trouble." I heard Sammy yell, "Down with the emperor" in return and saw Mr. Nizer roll his eyes toward heaven and clench his fist.

Mr. Fujimoto, who had been facing east all this time, now turned on his heel, dropped his hands to his side, and stared in front of him at the assembly. Every month I wondered whether he would ever speak to us after the ceremony. But today, just as in the past, he did not say a word as he left the stage and strode down the middle aisle to the door. I thought he hesitated in front of Sammy, and my heart jumped. What would he do? I wondered. I turned around to look at Sammy, who winked at me. Mr. Fujimoto kept going, followed by Mr. Nizer. The door slammed, and I could hear their voices outside. I couldn't hear any words—just Mr. Nizer's pleading tone and Mr. Fujimoto's harsh, explosive one. Mr. Borotkin slowly got up from his seat and in a tired and gentle voice told us about the school soccer game next week. Then we were dismissed.

The bell clattered and we rushed out in the cold morning toward the main building, our breath smoking in front of us. As we were settling down in our seats, Mr. Nizer walked in and announced that we were going to have a test in trigonometry. "Right now, so get out your pencils and papers." I could hear the irritation in his voice. Trigonometry was my most hated subject. I looked desperately at Sammy, who was the Trig Whiz of our class. Usually we knew ahead of time about a test, and Sammy, who sat in front of me, would lean toward the right so I could look at his paper and copy his answers. Today we weren't prepared, and I wondered if Sammy would remember to move his papers so I could see them. Otherwise, I would fail miserably.

I leaned toward Sammy and whispered, "Remember to let me see your paper."

Sammy turned his head slightly and in a mocking voice said, "I don't know if I want to share my answers with a baby who wears mittens around her neck." My heart sank. Mr. Nizer was in the back of the room, but at any moment he would come up front and hear us whispering.

"Please, Sammy, don't argue with me now."

"I'll do it if you cut those mitten strings. I don't help babies."

He stared at me with his black eyes, his wavy hair falling over his forehead. I love him, I thought. I really love him; not in a baby way, but in a grown-up way. I wanted to kiss him and touch his hair.

"I'll cut the mittens, I promise."

"Now," he insisted. "Right now you have to do it."

"With what?"

"Here's my penknife." He handed me his Boy Scout knife.

"Okay, okay," I said and cut through the string, wondering what my mother would say and how I could ever explain it to her.

"Good girl," whispered Sammy in a soft voice and pursed his lips in a kiss.

Brown Is the Color of
My Betar Uniform

BROWN IS THE color of earth, of trees and roots. Mix red and green together and you get brown. Say "brown" out loud and it fills the mouth, nestling into every nook. Brown is the color of my Betar uniform, made of scratchy, sturdy material, sewed by Mrs. Feldman, who lives on Dickenson Road. Once a pampered daughter in Russia, she is now a seamstress who, her mouth filled with pins, circles around me on her knees. The brown cap is worn rakishly to one side. When you see the boys and girls together, we are a sea of solid browns, a force of browns, more than the sum of our uniforms. The meetings are held in a long, bare building in the schoolyard, just a few feet away from the schoolhouse. The aim is to instill Zionism in us, to build dreams of transforming the banks of the Jordan into a Jewish state, to forever end the Diaspora. "Discipline is the bedrock of Betar," I hear it told from the pulpit by a fist-clenching man who stands on his tiptoes to add height to his small, compact body. In faraway China he flaunts his dream of the unborn state. My mind wanders as I look out of the window and instead of a far-off blooming desert and happy, suntanned kibbutzniks, I see the bald, bare, brown trees and swirling leaves of a cold November day. I dream of the quarterly Betar dances held in the meeting room, of a uniform clinging to my seemingly never-about-to-bud body. Perhaps if I tighten the black leather belt or breathe in deeply, perhaps if I use my mother's cologne, I will be asked this time to step out onto the recently swept floor to dip and curve in front of the less fortunate girls who stare vacantly ahead, glued-on smiles pasted on yearning, lightly lipsticked mouths. Perhaps this next time, Zionism, tempered by a tight-fitting uniform, will create a thing of beauty—rich, pungent, deep brown beauty.

Red and Yellow

ON THE STREET I was dangerously aware of China. She hung delicately, a gossamer around me. How was I to avoid hearing the tinkle of the outdoor barber's bell, the soft padding of the rickshaw man's stride, his labored breathing? How was I not to smell the pungent aroma of garlic, to avert my eyes from the dead beggar wrapped in rags? How was I to ignore the parading Japanese soldiers by the wire-strung barricades, the Japanese flag on top of the roof of the old American Embassy?

Being my father's daughter, I dreamt of other things. Of Joseph, the new boy in class, who had attracted my attention by putting my pigtails into an ink bottle and then grinning at me. Was this love, love, love? I wondered. In my diary last night I had given him a code name—27. I named all my loves by numbers, not sequentially but randomly, with abandon. My diary was like a spy's notebook, full of codes, ambiguities, circumventions, hints. Nothing was as it really was.

Walking to school one morning, I felt a strange, fruity taste in my mouth, an unidentified ooze slithering through my body. Usually at this hour students filtered slowly in, still sleepy, the boys punching each other lackadaisically, as if by rote, and the girls, gentle, like closed flowers, not showing their colors.

But today as I got closer to the school I heard a low roar, as if a hundred mosquitoes were dancing. "My" Joseph was pawing like a heated stallion. He was pointing to something written on the wall, something I

could not see. The roar deepened as I moved forward. Girls were droop-
ing and leaning on each other as if some mysterious disease had struck
them down. They pillared against each other like sagging posts in distress.
In the back of my throat an unfamiliar tickle was forming itself.

The roar now sounded like a low, persistent moan, punctuated by ag-
gressive boy shouts.

"Let's get them."

"They can't do this to us. Writing on our walls."

"Be careful, Joseph, be careful." A delicate girlish voice.

"Let's go, Joseph," shouted a husky adolescent male.

"Did anyone see them?" A bevy of voices. "How dare they do this?"

"I saw them. I know who they are."

Out of the moaning mass of girl voices, Rosa's now separated itself. The
group mobilized around her, sucking her information like honey from a
queen bee. A small quiver of jealousy spread its tentacles in me. How was
it that she was always the center of attention? And why was she so tall all
of a sudden? A Joan of Arc, Helen of Troy, Cleopatra. Woman storming
the barricades. I realized as I got closer that she was standing on a stool.

"They're from the Russian school. I know one. His name is Vassily
Tiomkin," Rosa said with grand self-assertion.

"And the others?"

"Don't know. But if we can get Vassily we'll get the rest. They run in
a pack."

"Then what are we waiting for?" Joseph said, echoing Rosa, looking at
her with covetous admiration. Together they are unbeatable, I thought to
myself. Zeus. Electra.

The crowd surrounding me had a steamy aliveness, a mixture of the
heady perfume used by some of the girls with the musky smell of boys becoming men. I was feeling light-headed, sparks detonating deep inside me
and spiraling to the surface. Someone poked me in the back. "Look, look."

In front of me giant letters covered the school wall from top to bottom.
DJID, DIRTY JEW. Crude, uneven, slanting letters in vile bile yellow. DJID.
Written by the enemy. Against the gray brick wall they throbbed and pul-
sated. It was the word that none of us ever used. The forbidden word. In
their mouths the word sat spattered by spit, in their belly it found its birth,
in their throat it matured and became a sound. The word reduced me,

sent spiky shivers of ancestral fear, accelerated my heartbeat. Suddenly I hated yellow. Everything yellow. Even the sun.

Someone was furiously scrubbing the wall with a wet rag. A girl from a younger class, a child really, with two red braids hanging down her back. They were now bobbing up and down as she went about her mission with messianic zeal. At her feet stood a steaming bucket of water with soapsuds.

The child toiler had to stand on her tiptoes to reach the high places. I watched her diligence, her dedication. My head whirled, and the unfamiliar tickle was now turning into an avalanche of nausea, followed by a jerking sensation in my stomach. My knees buckled and I slid to the ground, upsetting the soap-water bucket. The child screamed, "Look what you did!" Her voice squeaked in high registers. "Now I'm going to have to get another pail." Other voices, high above me, were yelling, "Get up" and "We've got work to do." I could not match the voices to the dim faces floating above me. "Let's get Mrs. Bialik. She'll know what to do," someone yelled. Then there was quiet.

I couldn't get up. There was a strangeness in my belly, putty in my limbs and an expanding feeling in my chest. I watched the yellow words disappear, the wet rag dripping yellow ooze on the ground. Beside it now a new spot appeared. It was red and getting bigger. Lazily I wondered why the child was mixing red with yellow. Red and yellow make orange, I thought, and somehow this gave me comfort. I was still on the ground, feet stepping all over me. An army of feet. The red spot was oozing out of me, I realized. "I've been shot," I screamed, but the words stuck like giant claws in my throat. Surprisingly, there was no pain. I had read about people being shot and not knowing it until later. I could see the headlines in the *North China Times*, "Riots at the High School," "Student Caught in Cross Fire between Japanese Police and Locals," or "The Pogroms Are Not Over." My father would hide the paper from me, even if I asked to see it. "It's too unpleasant. Don't bother yourself with it," he would say. My mother might mutter vague words meant to soothe. It would all have a high feeling of delicacy and abstinence.

Two pairs of neatly laced black shoes jarred my reverie. One, topped by sturdy pre-nylon stockings leading to a sensible Scotch tartan skirt, belonged to Mrs. Bialik, the school secretary, the other to Mr. Nizer, the jowly-faced schoolteacher.

"Get up," said Mrs. Bialik, offering me her hand for leverage. I looked into her eyes swimming behind thick glasses. Her face lacked definition. It sagged uncertainly into the folds of her neck, which splayed downward toward her soft, droopy shoulders. "Get up," Mrs. Bialik urged again.

Joseph and his band of combat siblings were preparing to leave. The girls delicately waved their scarves as if sending them off on a crusade. They were bunched around Joseph like eager ladies-in-waiting. Even the child worker was in the throng, clinging to Joseph's arm with diminutive passion. I got up unsteadily, drenched with sweat. No one was paying any attention to me.

Mr. Nizer was saying something, but his first words could not be heard. He shook his jowls, as if imitating a tiger about to pounce; but he was no tiger and the words came out meek and trembly.

"Stop this nonsense," he squeaked at the throng. "Get back to class."

Joseph, who towered over the teacher by at least three inches, spoke with great authority.

"We're going to get the bastards, and no one is stopping us."

"I am stopping you," squealed Mr. Nizer, his voice now in the high tenor range.

Feet apart, hands on his hips, Joseph smiled at the principal and his subjects knowingly and then started walking away. His band, suddenly mesmerized into action, brushed past Mr. Nizer, close enough to disarray the principal's thinning hair. He stood with his meaty white hands hanging ineffectively by his sides. Turning longingly to the girls still waving their scarves to the disappearing boys, he seemed to ask at least for their approval. But they too ignored him. I watched as he picked up the rag and began to scrub the wall, dripping puddles of suds. The child worker stood by without offering any help.

I hungered to stay with the girls, to be close to Rosa, to be part of their squealy, fragrant passions, but Mrs. Bialik took me by the arm and led me away. When she brought me to the bathroom, I was sure I would have to wait there for the town doctor to examine my wounds. There still was no pain, but a pushing and pulling discomfort deep in my groin.

"Look at your dress," said Mrs. Bialik. I looked.

"Turn around and look behind you," she ordered.

Back there, folded into the pile of my light-green-velvet skirt was a red spot. Why was it in the back, when I had been shot in the belly?

"You're," she hesitated. "You're . . . having . . . the . . . period."

When I was silent, she said, "This is your first time, isn't it?"

I nodded. I had looked up the word when an older cousin had told me one day I would have blood coming out of me regularly. Menstruation. Menorrhagia. Monthly. Period. My favorite had been "menarche." So I am in menarche, I thought.

"You probably should go home."

"I'd rather stay in school, if it's all right." I said. "I want to find out if Joseph and the boys beat Vassily up." I now deeply desired to see blood other than my own.

Mrs. Bialik frowned slightly and sighed. "He's a hothead, that Joseph. The worst thing to do in these circumstances is to start a fight."

"But if we don't fight, they'll keep writing . . ." I couldn't say the word. "And anyway, they started it." I was pleased with the way I was sticking up for Joseph. "I stood up for you," I imagined telling him one day. He would stare at me without saying a word, but I would know he was pleased.

"Words don't kill. It's just a word. We have to put up with it. This way, the two communities will be at each other's throats. All the time. We just have to put up with it," she said in a dry, professorial manner.

"But why?" I asked with newfound stubbornness. I wanted some fire from this adult, some dismay, a demonstration of outrage. She gave me none of it, well-versed as she was in aloof efficiency.

"Adolescents are hotheads—they have to be cooled down. Otherwise there would be . . ."—Mrs. Bialik threw up her hands—"chaos." She spat out the word "chaos" as if it stung her mouth.

I hailed this surge of emotion from the tightly booted Mrs. Bialik with glee. She was upset. Maybe now we could talk. In the quiet of the girls' bathroom with its peeling green walls, its black and white-gray tiles, and curtainless, gaping windows, I had possibly found an adult who could give me something warm, something vibrant. But Mrs. Bialik delicately wiped her mouth as if to expunge any trace of her last words. She glanced at her watch, tapped it lightly as if to make time go faster, and stared at me vaguely.

"You'll need a . . . napkin," she said delicately as she walked to a locked box on a shelf and took out a piece of cloth and some safety pins. "Put this on. Then you can wait here or in the hall. Until your dress dries." She hurried out. Perhaps she had been instructed to stay with the newly menstruating students for no more than five minutes. Duty done. My silent hopes for a chat were now shattered.

I looked at the back of my dress and found that the dampness had hardened into a cakey brown spot. Water only exaggerated its offensiveness. I walked out into the hall, where the silence was tomblike. Squeamish about sitting down on the stain, I walked around, staring at the dusty skeleton in the corner, the furled Japanese flag taken out only for assemblies, the shelves filled with *Encyclopaedia Britannica*, circa 1920. I could hear the hum of voices coming from the upstairs classes.

Then the front door was slammed open and Joseph rushed in, eyes flashing, lips sweating, the smell of battle hanging on him like a regal cape. His "men" strutted behind, swashbuckling with newly minted pride. A pack of girls brought up the rear, shrill and dizzy with laughter. Mr. Nizer trailed behind, breathing with difficulty, sweat running down his pasty cheeks. He is so out of place, I thought to myself. He doesn't belong. And neither do I, I thought with tear-filled eyes. I clung close to a protective wall, feeling that otherwise I would get mowed down.

"We got them. And gave them a thrashing. A victory, a true victory," Joseph pronounced regally. Was he speaking to me? I couldn't tell. There was a kingly grandeur to his gestures, and he seemed to have grown at least three inches since I'd last seen him. I yearned to be in his retinue and stepped out cautiously, but they swept by me, floating upstairs like a flock of shiny butterflies. "Hoorah!" yelled the boys. "Bravo, bravo," tinkled the girls.

"Go up now, it's time for class," growled Mr. Nizer. "Stop dawdling. Go on." I climbed the stairs, feeling heavy and loutish.

By three-thirty in the afternoon the red spot on my green-velvet dress had not disappeared. It was now an ugly earth-colored smudge. Between my legs the soft cloth had hardened and was chafing against my thighs. There was a feeling of movement down there, a sense of new things happening. But Joseph was not going to be one of the new events in my life. He had swept past me. He and his band of followers were like a flock of large, light, and buoyant birds. I, a small, nested bird, had no place in their world.

My walk home was sluggish. In the alley the yellow words had been thoroughly scrubbed away. Not a trace of them. Had they ever been there? My redness was still with me, in me, part of me. My menarche.

Two blocks from home I stopped dead in my tracks. How was I ever going to tell them about it? About the red and the yellow? About the word on the wall and my menarche? Two monumental events in one day. Was I finally going to have to violate the sacred code of silence, the inviolate agreement? I rolled various phrases around in my mind. "I started my menarche." Too crude. Too harsh. "I need a new cloth because I am menstruating." Too indelicate. "I thought I was shot this morning because I found myself in a pool of blood." Too melodramatic and frightening. Besides I would have to use the word "shot" and that was an inadmissible word. "Someone painted DJID on our schoolyard wall. In yellow." The only noncontroversial word was "yellow." Otherwise the whole sentence violated the contract. Maybe I could just use the words "yellow" and "red," hoping that they could decode the meaning. I daydreamed that my mother would look at me knowingly, not say a word, and bring out a fresh new cloth. My father would look at me lovingly and say, "You're growing up." Then he would pat me on the head.

I walked into the apartment, glancing around to see if both were there. "Did you have a good day at school?" asked my father.

"I cut myself and need some new bandages." I blurted out.

My father frowned. He hated the sight of blood and never looked at any of my cuts. There was the time he fainted in the doctor's office when I was given a shot for minor surgery. "He's delicate. Very sensitive, your father," the doctor had said.

"Ask your mother. She'll have some bandages. That's her department."

I was tempted to try out "red" and "yellow" and see if he understood. But a shimmering Do Not Disturb sign hung in the silence. He looked so contented reading his book, smiling to himself.

My mother, equally preoccupied with her knitting, suggested I look in the second drawer of the hall closet for bandages. "I'll come in a minute to see how you're bandaging yourself."

When she came in a few minutes later I told her the cut was superficial and that I had bandaged it myself. I showed her my bandaged finger and she did not question me.

The cloth between my legs lay like a cold stone. Something had to be done. Rummaging in the Chinese chest that held my clothes, I came across a bundle of neatly folded and faded soft towels. Lying next to them was a package of pins. I had never seen them before, or perhaps I had but had not known their use. Without a doubt they were for me. I held them close as newfound friends.

I wrote in my diary later that day: "Saw 27 today. He was quite a hero, but probably never will really see me. There were huge yellow words on the wall at school. Bad words. Had my first red spot. This has been a day of colors. Red and yellow make orange. It has been an important day. May 24, 1942."

Taking a Bath

DURING THE WAR hot water is a steamy dream, a vapory image seldom within reach, a deep, low-bellied hunger aching to be satisfied. During the war coal is scarce and what there is produces meek heat. Most of it is saved for the giant gobbler, the stove. Pipes that once brought a cascade of hot water lie glumly unused. For hand and face washing a pot of water is boiled on the stove, and we take turns washing ourselves in the same pot. By the time my father's turn comes around, the water is lukewarm.

There is never enough coal to heat water for a bath, and as the winter months unfold I am preoccupied with hot-water thoughts. Sometimes I think I could give up chocolate wafers, Florida oranges, sugar, and even friendships for a daily hot bath. I dream of a long procession of baths all filled to the brim with sudsy, boiling water.

Twice a month, on Fridays, my dream is realized at the Drisins'. Their apartment house is owned by someone who still provides delicious hot water on demand, and we are privileged to be beneficiaries of this largesse. How long it will last, my mother says, is not clear. Rumor is that the Drisins' apartment house will soon join the ranks of the unheated.

But as of now, at the Drisins', there is no need to save water. There is no need to work for it, no need to prepare and coax the stove. At the Drisins', a turn of the spigot and a column of steamy water jettisons itself like a fiery plume into the bath. Above it a cloud of vapor rises upward, and soon I am surrounded by steam and vapor and water. Boundaries melt, walls shimmer, mist envelops. Up to my neck I lie in a cocoon of heat, limbs melting, skin a velvety shroud. The chatter of voices in the dining room and the clatter of dinner preparation come to me from a great distance. Here I am the Heat Goddess and the world is centuries away.

Carte Blanche

"SCRATCH A RUSSIAN and you will always find an anti-Semite. Even in China, 1945."

"Some of them are all right. Have a friend, Vera Smirnova. Never, never has she said anything anti-Semitic. At least not to me."

"Well, maybe there is an exception to every rule."

"No, I disagree. There are no exceptions. And when they're drunk, they're totally impossible. 'Christ killers,' that's what they always call us when they're drunk."

"Imagine how her mother feels. Her marrying a Russian. Poor woman, what a disgrace."

"Thank God it never happened in our family."

"They say his father is half Jewish, but the old man denies it, and they all go to church. Regularly. And he's never worked permanently."

"I would die having to go into a room with an icon. In their homes, every room has an icon. Gives me the chills, just thinking about it."

"Must admit he's good-looking. Brutish and vulgar, sometimes drunk. But good-looking."

"And she's a lovely girl. Hardworking. Has provided for her mother and has been the mainstay in that family. A lovely Jewish girl. And now this. What a tragedy. Marrying that Walter Denko."

As I walked through the streets of Tientsin, in the summer of 1945, those words hovered over rooftops, seeped through the cracks in the sidewalks, and whistled in the summer breeze. It was my Aunt Mary they were speaking of when I came into the room. People averted their eyes, strangling their words like wounded birds into their collars and shoulders.

I adored my Aunt Mary. I used to watch her put on her lipstick in the kitchen of Grandmother's house, where she claimed the light was the best, rounding her lips into a little cupid red bow. I loved her round, soft body, her upswept little nose, her blue-gray eyes. When I looked into the mirror I was always surprised and baffled by my long nose, furrowed brow, and short legs that made me look like a gnome. Once I took Aunt Mary's rouge and lipstick and tried to use it. The results were disastrous. The face that looked back at me from the mirror was a clown's face. It was a mystery I could not understand.

Aunt Mary and Grandmother lived in the corner house at Victoria Road and Colony Street, where Grandmother rented rooms. For many years they slept in the closet beneath the staircase, where only in the very center could anyone stand upright. Later they moved into a room, and my grandmother would apologetically murmur, "I know we could get a good price for this room, but what a pleasure to have an entire room at one's disposal, one where you can stand up straight in all the corners."

Grandmother and Aunt Mary came from a small, predominantly Jewish village near Moscow, and during the Revolution of 1917 they fled east toward the Pacific, joining my mother in Tientsin. They traveled by train for many days. Once the train stopped inexplicably. They waited for hours in terror while pimply adolescent Russian boys in ill-fitting uniforms conducted clumsy searches of their belongings. From my Aunt Mary they took a beloved teddy bear, hoisting it on their shoulders like prize booty.

Aunt Mary often took me shopping, and we would stroll down Victoria Road, my hand firmly in hers, looking at shop windows. My favorite was Whiteways and Company, a giant emporium, the first floor of which was filled almost exclusively with a wide assortment of toys.

"Anything you want is yours," she would say merrily as I stood, nose pressed to the cool glass, our reflections shimmering amid the display of giant pandas and bears.

"Anything?" I asked, my heart beating with excitement.

"Yes, carte blanche. Anything at all."

"Can I have the teddy bear? And paper dolls?"

"Of course."

"AND the kaleidoscope?" I squealed with desire for the magic tube that turned the world into flashing cubes and spheres.

"Of course."

"Really, really, really?" I shrieked, pretending not to believe her and stretching the moment of delicious uncertainty taut like a rubber band until it popped, and we stepped into the cavernous room stuffed with toys.

Once I asked her if she ever bought "carte blanche" for anyone else. She looked at me squarely, kissed me on the top of my nose, and said, "I buy things for your cousins, but carte blanche is only for you." As she pressed me to her, I inhaled the sweet lavender cologne she wore, my heart welling with joy. I was special, long nose and stumpy legs. I was special.

She met Walter Denko at Rivkin and Company, where she worked as a secretary to Mr. Joseph Rivkin, a seedy, cross-eyed man who pinched all women in a desultory manner, propelled by habit rather than desire. Mr. Rivkin was in the fur business. Often late for work, he routinely forgot to pay salaries and smoked pungent cigars, dropping ashes all over the office furniture and carpet. Aunt Mary was totally dedicated to him. When he was late for appointments with prospective buyers, she made excuses for him. When the checks were late or bounced, she forgave him.

One day Mr. Rivkin breezed into the office with a man he introduced as Walter Denko. "We've made a deal," he said, winking at Mary with his wild eye. "Walter is going to take a new shipment of furs off my hands. I'll take you both out for lunch. To celebrate."

Three months later Walter and Mary decided to marry. Grandmother wept and threatened suicide. "How will I ever be able to hold my head up in the community? Marrying a Russian Orthodox! I spent my life on you and this is how you repay me? This is a sin. God will punish you."

Grandmother moaned and cried and even promised Mary a room of her own, but my Aunt Mary remained firm. The rest of the family gave up their appeals in light of her breathtaking resolve. She was immovable, a magnificent white column of passion and love.

From the beginning Walter frightened me. Around his thick neck, he wore a gold cross that glistened in the sunlight. He strode through our apartment like an unleashed bull, causing china to rattle in my mother's cupboard. Every Sunday, without fail, he went to the Russian Orthodox church across the river. I had never been allowed to go there. It was off limits, an enemy camp.

When he patted me on my head, I felt the hard calluses of his palm irritating my scalp. His hugs were giant crushes against his rib cage, leaving me gasping for air. He was bulky, yet strangely graceful on the dance floor. I grudgingly had to admit Aunt Mary was right every time when she said, "Just look at him. He dances like a god."

I felt betrayed by Aunt Mary's consuming interest in Walter. Our walks on Victoria Road had become irregular, and even when we took them she seemed preoccupied and distant. Sometimes she would dash into our house, saying, "No time for a walk this week, so I got you these." She would thrust presents into my hands, but I refused to open them and stacked them up in my room.

"Stop moping and grow up," my mother said. "They're getting married and that's that."

"But why? I hate him. He is so . . . so different. And he's taken her away from me."

"She loves him. That's why. Unconditional love. Love despite and in spite of everything."

"What's that?"

"Someday you'll understand."

"Last week he made me eat everything on my plate, and he kept piling on more food and he kept yelling, 'Eat, eat.' He was drunk, I know it. You know what I did when he wasn't looking? I ran to the bathroom and vomited. I hate him. I hate him."

In their wedding picture, Walter bulges out of his tuxedo, his wavy blond hair cascading around his massive forehead, his powerful hands clasped tightly as if to restrain them from possible violence. He stares straight ahead. Aunt Mary looks soft and radiant. The rest of the family, bunched together to the side like a pack of abandoned puppies, gaze off into the distance. I heard new words in the streets now, echoed in the treetops and carried on the wings of birds.

"Well, it's done with. For better or worse. They're married."

"The poor mother."

"I heard she wept for days."

"But now she has accepted it."

"What else can she do, poor woman? A daughter is a daughter."

"I would have killed myself. A Russian Orthodox son-in-law."

"And he's still not working—living off of her."

"What will they do about the children?"

"Don't think ahead."

"I would die if my daughter married a Russian. Absolutely die."

"Thank God it isn't your daughter. Or mine."

"Love. There's nothing you or I can do about love."

"They say she adores him. Love has no reason."

A year later Mary and Walter celebrated their first anniversary at his parents' house. It was below zero outside, but the two rooms in the tiny apartment were so tightly packed with guests that the windows sweated moisture and the potbellied stove was left unattended. The overstuffed furniture had been pushed against the walls, the gleaming samovar and a giant Victrola were squeezed into a corner, and the Singer sewing machine, moved into the dim hallway, caused a tremendous traffic jam between the connecting rooms. The large dining room table groaned with food. Russian pierogi filled with cabbage and meat, purple eggplant salad in stemmed glass dishes, smoked herring, gefilte fish and chopped liver, a ham with deep orange glaze, stewed fruit, walnut cake, vodka and wines in crystal carafes. The candlelight from the icon in the corner cast flickering shadows.

Dirty dishes were passed back to the kitchen, and Cook wove his way in and out of the crowd, bringing replenishment, continuously piling the table with more food, so that no dish ever stood empty. I ate gefilte fish with sturdy dollops of horseradish that made my eyes water. The steamy, smoky room, the hum of voices, my favorite people making music together, their dark heads glistening like shiny disks over the piano, filled the very crevices of my being with joy. I was content. We were united again. Never mind that the Byzantine icon flickered in the corner. If I closed my eyes I could will it away or pretend it was just an ordinary candle. I could even pretend that Walter didn't exist.

Then, slicing through the rich melody of their voices and through my ecstatic reverie, I heard Walter's loud voice. He was drunk, his square face glistened with sweat, his hair damp on his forehead. "Play 'Volga Boat-men,'" he bellowed at my father. I watched him moving from the door toward the piano, careening through the crowd. He held a glass filled with vodka, drops of which splattered guests standing in his way. "Goddamn it, play 'Volga Boatmen'!" My father hastened to oblige. Walter grabbed a woman, crushing her to his chest. "To friendship. To love. To God," he blared, raising his glass high. The woman tried to wriggle out of his grasp, but he hung on to her. Tears rolled down his flushed cheeks as he sang "The Volga Boatmen." The woman lay limp against his chest, her mouth slightly open, like a beached fish, her eyes pleading. Walter sang on, oblivious of her. He sang in a maddened frenzy, the words spilling out incomprehensibly.

"Walter, dear, perhaps another song." My Aunt Mary's voice was gentle. "'Volga Boatmen' is so . . ." she searched for words, "so . . . uh . . . mov-ing. It always upsets you."

He glared at her, pushed the woman in his hold away from him. She scampered away like a mouse reprieved from a cat's paw. "In my house, I sing when and what I want," he said through clenched teeth, the veins in his forehead visibly throbbing, his eyes bloodshot.

"Yes, yes," shouted the guests. "How about another song? How about 'Some of These Days' or 'Lullaby of Broadway'?"

Walter swayed from side to side, pawing the floor with his feet like a maddened bull. "This is my anniversary, I will sing what I want to sing. Keep playing, piano player, don't stop."

"Darling, how about some food?" Aunt Mary spoke in her soft, ap-peasing voice and offered him a piece of bread thick with eggplant paste.

Walter knocked the bread from her hand. Eggplant dribbled down her dress. There was a hush in the room, voices quieting like bird wings stopped in midflight. The grandfather clock struck seven, the sonorous booms echoing in the quiet room. My parents stared at Walter with a look of helpless bewilderment on their faces.

"You Yids, always horning in." Walter's face was a mask of rage. "Get out, all of you. Get out of my way. I want to sing alone." Tears ran down his face. "More vodka," he yelled. "More. More. More. To mother Russia. Down with the Yids."

The guests were stunned, hushed. My cheeks were flushed with humiliation. I felt everyone in the room was looking at me—the niece, by marriage, of Walter Denko. "For heaven's sake, do something, don't just stand there!" The words erupted in my head as I looked at my timid family, pain etching their faces. "Please," I pleaded silently. "Please. Do something." But nothing happened.

With great effort, as if after a long illness, I got up and walked toward Walter. He towered above me. "You unwanted horrid fiend." My words seared my tongue like hot coals, filling my chest cavity until I felt I would explode. "You unwanted hideous fiend."

Walter looked like a deflated balloon, all saggy. Tears rolled down his cheeks. Aunt Mary touched me tenderly on my shoulder. "Sha," she crooned to me, "sha."

Turning to Walter, she said, "Darling, why don't you go into the next room and rest? You are very tired. Very tired indeed."

"Yes, dear. Tired," he repeated after her.

She led Walter by the hand, the crowd parting to make way for them. I could hear her cooing words of endearment. She put her head on his shoulder. Just before the dim hallway swallowed the two figures, I saw Walter put his arm around her waist and she, around his. For a moment they were bathed in light.

The festivities continued without them until midnight. I felt utterly exhausted and stretched out on the maroon couch, ignored by the guests and my family. It was as if my rage had dropped like a stone to the bottom of a deep pond without even a ripple left to show its existence. What had I hoped for? Approval? Accolades? Everyone pretended nothing had happened. My father went back to his piano playing. Aunt Mary and Mother sang. I felt a bomb had exploded, a bomb visible only to me. I fell asleep and dreamt that Aunt Mary stood over a figure. She was crying. The figure was Walter. Aunt Mary turned to me and said, "In death a peaceful man . . . You were too hard on him. He needed time. You were too hard on him."

"Did you hear about the party?"
"I was there. When drunk, they're impossible."

"Still. A year married. It's a miracle. No one thought it would last. They've moved in with her mother."

"Can you imagine that? The poor woman with a Slav in her household. Under her very nose."

"And going to church every Sunday. Walks out of that Jewish household, in broad daylight, and crosses the river to his church."

"What one has to bear for one's daughters."

"Well, I couldn't do it."

"I hear she's given them the best room in the house."

The day of their move to Grandmother's house, I made sure I was there. Aunt Mary was at work and Walter executed the move single-handedly. He carried their furniture and other belongings up the two flights of stairs. Methodical and well organized, he whistled throughout the entire operation. At last he carried their cat, Archie, in and gently laid him on their huge bed with the blue satin bedspread embroidered with pink peacocks. I saw him hang the curtains and I watched him go out and bring back a huge bouquet of flowers, which he put in a vase on the nightstand. In a few hours their room looked as if they had always lived in it. Then Aunt Mary came home from work.

"Darling, how beautiful. Such gorgeous flowers."

"Nothing but the best for my princess."

Their voices rose and sank, whispered and cooed. Later that evening they went out arm in arm.

I was repelled by her blind love, her misplaced pride, her unswerving, devoted allegiance. Disgust whirled inside me. How she could love this uncouth, burly Russian was beyond my comprehension. His very blondness was an irritant to me.

"How come he is allowed to live at Grandmother's? I thought you all hated him."

"He is one of us now. Your Aunt Mary has chosen him. It is not for us to understand. It is for us to accept. Go find some friends and stop brooding about your Aunt Mary. Go."

Yes, it was time for me to find new friends, new attachments.

"I hear the nieces and nephews bought a ticket for Mary and she is going to visit them in America. She leaves São Paulo tomorrow."

"She and Walter have been together thirty years. Amazing."

"She still is the main support of the family, the sole provider. He just makes deals."

"Still, they have a Brazilian woman to do for them."

"Just like in China. They live here like they did there. Servants. Parties. Nothing changes."

"Nothing stronger than love, I guess."

"Me, I prefer a man who can support me. And doesn't get drunk."

"True. But the way she still looks at him. And he at her."

In 1973 Aunt Mary flew from Brazil to California to visit me. I was in the midst of a divorce. She was still soft, but heavier, and her hands had thickened with arthritis. She and Walter had been living in São Paulo since 1960.

"When can we go shopping?" she asked a few days after her arrival.

"Anytime," I said.

"Just like old times. Remember?"

"Now it's my turn to do carte blanche." We went to a big department store downtown, and I wanted to take her to the newly decorated outdoor lunchroom.

"First I want to buy Walter something. A leather jacket, like this one." She took out a folded, worn-out newspaper ad showing a burly young man in a leather jacket. "Walter still looks good," she said proudly. "He wears his years well. No one can believe he's almost sixty."

"But I want to take you to ladies' wear first." My voice was whiny with disappointment. Walter's unwanted shadow once again came between us, and a long-forgotten rage stirred inside me.

But Aunt Mary was adamant, and we were soon looking over the stock of leather jackets, my eyes smarting from the acrid smell. She pinched the material for softness, carefully examined the linings, and finally decided on one. After the saleslady rang up her purchase on the cash register, Aunt Mary said, "Now we can go and get dresses for me. Now that I have found something for Walter."

In the dress department her interest dissipated. "It's fine, wonderful," she said hastily and hardly looked at a dress I held out for her. We bought two that she didn't even try on. "I'm sure they'll fit," she reassured me. We decided to forget lunch, because suddenly she felt tired.

In the car she asked about my divorce. Why? How come? What for?

"We don't communicate," I struggled to explain something still fuzzy in my mind. "He wanted independence . . . his own space . . . I mean, he wanted to go his own way. And I . . . well, I wanted . . . a closer relationship . . . and we were always fighting about what was fair . . . who was doing his fair share in the marriage. Then there were women . . . sometimes. He just wasn't committed. I felt I was carrying most of the responsibilities . . . and he was just moody . . . all the time."

She stared at me in disbelief. "What is all this talk about fairness, independence, commitment? Marriage is not a business contract—fifty-fifty. I love Walter one hundred percent and I'm proud of it. And we don't ration it out or measure it. I give all the time, and giving is fulfillment in itself." She was staring at me with bright, shiny eyes, her lips quivering. "I love Walter for what he is, not what he could be."

"For heaven's sake, what is he?" I interrupted sharply.

"He's kind. He's caring. He loves imperfectly, but he loves. And he's mine."

"Is that enough?"

"Of course. I'm incomplete without him. Together we make one," she burst out as if in song. "We're one."

I was stunned by her white-hot passion. Perhaps that was the way to love; perhaps my marriage had died, sagging under a mountain of analysis and wordy miscommunications. I thought of the hours spent dissecting it, the years of bitter conversations that left me dry-mouthed and bone-weary. Hers is a blind love, an unqualified love, an obsession, I thought to myself. And yet, as I saw her tired but content and looking serene and plump as she snuggled into her seat holding on to the leather jacket, I found myself yearning for her fiery, consuming ardor.

I started to ask her how she survived the fire, but decided against it. Neither did I bring up the incident in 1947 at the party, which had haunted me through the years. She had, no doubt, fervently forgiven Walter his transgressions.

When she left a few weeks later, her small, battered carry-on bulged with clothes for Walter and little mementos for friends. She wouldn't let it out of her sight, clinging to it and insisting that it couldn't go baggage.

"You sure gave me carte blanche," she said just before we were separated
and she disappeared into the dark tunnel leading to the airplane.

"But you hardly bought anything for yourself."

"What's the difference? Walter and I, we're one. It was carte blanche for
the two of us." She gave me a hug. I smelled the familiar perfume, tears
stinging my eyes as she pushed me away from her.

She died several years later, under anesthesia during a minor elective
surgical procedure. We were all stunned, and Walter wrote that the light
had dimmed in his life.

Graduation Night at
Tientsin Jewish High

I STAND IN front of the mirror in my mother's bedroom, scowling at my-self, seeing how the two "worry marks," as my mother calls them, on my forehead close in on each other and thinking how ugly I am and how noth-ing, absolutely nothing, looks right, how my legs are too short and my rear end sticks out, how my nose is long, and how not even a built-in bra with bones that are now sticking into my flesh will give the illusion of breasts and how the pink georgette dress with yards of pink satin ribbons sewn in and the heart-shaped bodice and heart-shaped sleeves make my face look yellow, when my mother, who has been on her knees hemming my dress, says, "Darling, you look simply gorgeous. And stop scowling. You'll etch permanent worry marks, and we don't want that," she says as she looks up into the mirror and sees my reflection. I stop scowling, because I don't want to disappoint her and because I love her. She is so cute and filled in in all the right places and she always tells me how wonderful and gorgeous I am, even though she and Father surely must know, they just have to look to see that I'm ugly. Besides, I have to wear glasses, as if I didn't have enough trouble, but they both tell me I look "scholarly" and "artistic," which again I don't have the heart to tell them is the last thing I want to be. "Never make passes at girls who wear glasses" is a favorite song of Joe Pitkin's, and he always seems to sing it when I pass by him, and Joe is the one I'm in love with, but I never talk to him because he is always singing that song and I don't know if he is trying to tell me something or flirting

with me. My friend Rose says that boys sometimes flirt with girls by saying mean things to them, so maybe he is flirting with me.

We are getting ready for my high school graduation party, the tenth
graduation in the entire history of Tientsin Jewish High School, Tientsin,
China, which will be later on this evening, and my mother is putting the
finishing touches on me. My hair has been curled in rags all morning and
the rags are still in and they look funny bobbing up and down on my
shoulders while the rest of me is already so dressed up in my pink georgette dress, which was copied from a dress in a picture that my mother had
cut out from a 1940 *True Romance* magazine that she had when she was
trying to learn English and reading all the *True Romances* she could get her
hands on. She had taken the cutout to Mrs. Feldman, who is an incredible
seamstress and can make exact copies from pictures, and together my
mother and Mrs. Feldman decided that pink georgette was the best material and color.

I am going to the graduation party with my father and mother, which
is all right, but it would be decidedly better if I were going with Joe Pitkin,
or even Sammy Goldman. Several of the girls are going to arrive with their
boyfriends. They are the popular girls, which I would love to be, but I am
as far from popular as I am from the North Pole and will probably never
ever be popular, so I'm going to have to live with that. We are going in
Mr. George's car, which my father, who works for Mr. George, got for
the occasion. My father has worked for Mr. George for ages and says he
is Mr. George's "right hand," but I know he is just a glorified secretary and
does everything in the office that Mr. George wants, and I also know that
he worships Mr. George and even walks like him, and I hate to see him
be that way but I don't know quite how to tell him, because I love him
and I don't want to hurt his feelings. Anyway, Mr. George's car is going to
pick us up, so we will arrive in style. Which is much better than taking
the rickshaw to the party because my mother would probably want me to
sit on her lap to save fare, which is all right when I'm in my regular
clothes—though even then I am beginning to feel silly sitting on my
mother's lap in the rickshaw at my age—but in my first evening dress it
would be awfully embarrassing, which I couldn't tell them because I know
how little money we have and how we have to save, so having a car is a
great idea.

With Tsui, going to the club.

My mother puts on the finishing touches, ironing the hem of the long dress so that the georgette will fall smoothly to the ground, putting the hem on a chair beside me and making me turn around so she will get the full circle, making sure that all the snaps on the side are snugly secured and finally, at the very last minute, she unties the rags in my hair and the fat little sausage curls swing from my head, and then she brushes them all into a sweeping pageboy, and even I have to admit that things are looking better.

The last time I rode in a car was when my cousin Hazel came home from a diplomatic tour and we met her at the train station and an embassy car picked us all up. This is a big occasion. We drive down Victoria Road, turn left on Davenport Road, where the tallest building in town, the Elgin, which is eleven stories high, stands, and past my school, and we are in front of the Kunst Club, where my graduation party will take place. I am beginning to feel very nervous because after the diplomas are given out and the punch and cake are over, there will be a dance with an orchestra, and the graduation class is supposed to enjoy themselves—which is very unlikely for me since probably no one will ask me to dance and I'm going to have to sit there smiling until my mouth hurts and pretending I'm having a great time. My mother tells me I should be proud of myself because I am the youngest graduate in the class—apparently I broke the record by graduating at almost fifteen, but I keep reminding her that the only reason I graduated so early was that the school did not have form ten and form eleven, because there were no students for those two forms during the war, and I had a choice of staying on in form nine or skipping two grades and moving to form twelve, which I did, because my baby cousin Danny was in form nine and under no circumstances would I be caught dead with Danny in the same form. My mother tells me that despite everything, I am smart because I could keep up with the students in form twelve.

The Kunst auditorium is filled with balloons that are on streamers attached to the columns all along the big room, and in the middle of the room is a table with a sign that says, "Good Luck, Graduates." Around it are twenty-nine seats with our names on them, which is good, since I won't have to decide who I will sit next to (which of course if I had my choice would be Joe Pitkin, but then he usually sits with Fanny, so I would never get my chance even if I acted fast enough). As it turns out, I am seated next to David Fishman on my left and Sammy Goldman on my right, and both boys find hilarious things to say to the girls on their left and right, so I have no one to talk to and am miserable watching everyone else "enjoying" themselves. I look around the room and count the number of boys and girls. I have done this many times in my head, but now I do it once again to make sure that there are fifteen boys and fourteen girls, which means, numerically at least, that every girl has a chance at a boy partner, with even one "spare" boy, which makes me feel happier until the awful thought hits me that two of the boys, Mark and Donny, are on crutches after an accident last week when they bumped into each other at the skating rink, which means that there are now thirteen danceable boys and fourteen danceable girls, and I know, as sure as I know my name, that I will be the one without a partner.

I want the nondancing part of the graduation never to stop, I want to slow things down so that we will never come to the time when we have to go to the ballroom and start the dancing. Mr. Nizer, the principal, is onstage making his speeches about graduation and life ahead, and he is very boring, but I hope he will continue forever, making long speeches and have the graduates file by him several times. I am hoping that the cakes on

At the country club.

the table will be followed by other cakes and I look toward the kitchen
hoping, even seeing, more food coming through the swinging doors. I
pray for an earthquake that will suddenly, in one crashing, sweeping boom,
create a chasm so great between the auditorium and the ballroom that we
will all have to go home. I pray that a terrible rain will pummel the roof
of the ballroom and come down in great torrents, making the floor totally
undanceable. I heard that three years ago rain had indeed caused excessive
damage to the ballroom and it had stood empty for several months, but
they fixed it well, which according to my father was no mean feat, since it
took a lot of money and everyone in the community to chip in. So here
I am at the Kunst Club with a wonderful, dry roof over my head and not
a chance of any natural disaster coming my way.

Mr. Nizer finally finishes his speech and is followed by Mr. Perls, who
asks us all to stand up and file onstage to receive the diplomas, which
we do, but that doesn't take too long, and before I know it we are being
huddled into the dreaded ballroom. The graduates are all put in the middle
of the room, like animals in the zoo, and the first dance is announced
to be fathers and daughters and mothers and sons, so of course I dance

with my father, who is an excellent dancer and taught me how to tango and waltz, and he keeps telling me how proud he is of me. I don't have the heart to tell him that in the next few minutes he will see his "pride and joy" sitting in her usual wallflower place by the wall with no one to dance with. Of course, there always is "Ladies' Choice," and I intend to ask Joe Pitkin if Fanny or Mary or Rose hasn't already taken him.

I am led back to a row of chairs set up for the graduates, and they are so arranged that they are in full view of everyone in the ballroom, so that I am going to have to grit my teeth and face the whole world sitting alone in my chair, because Donny and Mark fell on the rink, which made my chances to be a danceable graduate zero. I resign myself to my awful fate and hear the start of the second dance. They are playing my favorite song, which is "Bye, Bye, Blackbird," which my mother often sings at home while my father plays the piano. Joe and Fanny are the first to start the dance, and I watch them doing a fast fox-trot with several fancy swing-out steps and Fanny is laughing and throwing her head back and Joe looks so absolutely gorgeous in his new blue suit. Then Rose follows with Dmitri, and the whole line of chairs, which is where I and all the girls have been sitting, empties as boy after boy comes to get his girl. And in a few minutes there is just me and a long line of chairs. I wish my dress were black so I could blend into the wall, but I stick out like a pink pimple and everyone in the entire room can see. I slouch into my chair, hoping to make myself small. My mother and father wave to me from the far end of the room and I wave back, thinking now you know about your precious daughter, the number one wallflower of the year, for the whole town to see, and all the heart-shaped pink georgette bodices and rag curls aren't going to make one bit of difference. I am beginning to feel cold and heavy and don't know what to do with my hands, which seem monstrously large and conspicuous, and I have even given up smiling and I'm scowling and my two worry marks are on my forehead and I don't care.

Then I look up and find myself looking into the eyes of Moses Guber, who is standing about ten feet away from me. Now Moses is a ninth former and is here only because his brother is graduating with me. Moses is my height, which means he is exceptionally small for a boy, and he has red hair that stands on edge around his head and he has freckles all over him—I mean all over—and he wears the most hideous glasses, and he is now staring at me. Just great, I think to myself. He's going to ask me for a dance, and I will be the only graduating twelfth former dancing with a ninth former, and on top of it all, we will be the smallest couple on the floor, and the ugliest, and everyone in the whole town will know that the pride and joy of my parents is not only ugly and a wallflower but that the only boy she could get to dance with her is also the ugliest and the smallest and not even a senior. I want to run away, but there is a wall behind me, a crowd of parents to my left, and the dancing seniors in front of me, and I feel trapped. I look up again, and Moses is now only five feet away but moving toward me with a sureness I cannot stop. His small, piglet eyes are staring at me with determination, and as he gets real close I see that his brow is sweaty. I put my head down and see a pair of well-polished shoes in front of me, which surprises me because Moses is ordinarily such a mess, but today his shoes are really spiffy. He stands in front of me and does not say anything, just keeps staring at me, and I look up and see my parents beaming and I look at Moses and say, "Are you asking me to dance?" and he nods his head and I stand up and put one hand on his shoulder and the other into his hand, which is sweaty and has several bumps or warts, and he smells of medicines because his father owns the local pharmacy and Moses is always behind the counter, and he steers me into the center of the ballroom, where everyone is heads taller than both of us, and I feel hot shame and anger, and yet there is my favorite "Bye, Bye, Blackbird" music and I give it a whirl.

III. *The War Is Over*

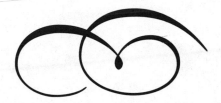

Tuna, Corn, and Hershey's Kisses

FOR HOURS I and a bevy of expectant, giggly girls, dressed in flowery hazy-dazy chiffon dresses, sit on the steps of the Astor House hotel waiting for the conquerors. The war is over, and the American Marines Third Amphibious Corps is said to be on its way. It will come from places whose names fit awkwardly in our mouths. Guadalcanal, Iwo Jima, Guam. The population of boys in my town will balloon to giant proportions. Unrequited love, a pastime I have indulged in for years, can now take its place in history, shoved back into the folklore of childhood. I am ready for real love.

The August day is steamy, and clothes cling titillatingly to our straining bodies. We lengthen our necks, giraffelike, to see beyond corners and around bushes, but for hours Victoria Road is filled only with watchers, mainly eager adolescent girls. There are some boys in the crowd. They lean heavily against trees, fences, and walls, perhaps realizing that their undisputed reign is about to be over. Together we nested in the cocoon of war, growing into our adolescence, preoccupied more with the strange new rumblings of our sexuality than with the exigencies of battle. Now peace is bursting in on us. New alliances. New loves.

"They're coming, they're coming." An expanding roar rustles the crowd, stiffens our moist dresses, tightens our yearning muscles. "They're coming."

The first mammoth tanks, like colossal celestial beings, laboriously part the now hushed crowd. Spinwheel firecrackers explode in my head. I want to drop down on my knees, have visions of genuflecting in some ancient ritual while screaming and rending my clothes. I hold hands with a friend and feel her fingernails digging into the palm of my hand. She digs deeper and deeper until blood squirts out in a tiny rivulet, but I feel no pain.

Gods sit on top of the tanks, dressed in rich umber khaki. They throw their hats in the air. They sing wild songs. They reach down and grab any young girl brave enough to climb their magic vessel.

In a pack of screaming girls I run toward the moving flotilla, waiting to be snatched up and held close to some uniform still fresh with the smell of war. I touch the cold, pulsating steel, I hear a steady rumbling coming from its innards. A voice yells, "Catch!" Something glints in the heat of the afternoon, something falls into my hands. I am surrounded by silvery objects. One melts in my hand. Another is firm with hard edges.

I hold a can of tuna, a can of creamed corn, and pellets of Hershey's chocolate kisses. A young soldier with the face of Ronald Coleman, or Tyrone Power, or all those gorgeous movie stars put together grins at me and his is the most beautiful smile I have ever seen. "More coming," he yells and I shriek back, "More, more and more," as I am pelted with drippy Hershey bars and almost knocked over by flying cans.

The Leaving

ON NOVEMBER 11, 1948, a crowd gathers on the Bund to watch those of us about to start our long journey to America. We will board the LST (Landing Ship Tank), which will first take us from Tientsin to Tsingtao. From there we will take the SS *General Butler* and head east for California. The anticipated time of the journey is unclear. The Pacific Ocean has been reported to be unseasonably choppy and violent. There is talk of storms.

It is a gloomy wintry evening, misty fog obscuring large portions of the Bund. The crowd is quiet, their voices muffled, their motions slow, as if movement is a painful endeavor, as if conservation of energy is to be achieved at all costs. Passengers huddle close to their suitcases and trunks, some slumped over their baggage. Friends and relatives form tight little protective knots around these crumpled figures, like silent sentinels at a lonely vigil. The fate of the ones left behind is uncertain. The fate of those of us who are leaving is also unclear. What is there to say under these circumstances? One can only witness.

I sit on our trunk, the kind that opens up into two wardrobe compartments, which my mother and I have filled chock-full with clothes, bedding, and mementos. She stands next to it. In it are my diaries and early compositions, written in a delicate hand, and all my watercolor paintings. In it are my aqua brocade Chinese jacket and my pink georgette high school graduation dress. In it are the crystal given to my parents for their wedding, the silver vase intricately carved to look like a basket, and the

*On a visit
to Peking.*

heavy book given by Czar Nicholas II to my grandfather. In it is my life
of nineteen years.

Only the American Marines, guardians of the bulky gray LST, are in motion. They are young, sinewy, and frisky. They bustle, commanding the
wharf as if it is yet another battleground and they the conquering heroes.
They are awaiting orders to board this motley group waiting patiently for
departure—American citizens returning home with the approach of the
Communists, people with long-awaited entry visas to the United States, and
an assortment of refugees seeking political asylum. The young Americans
chatter, puff endless Camels, and squat on tawny haunches drinking Cokes.

In the middle of this deadly calm, except for the rambunctious Americans, I find myself consumed by a column of red heat that seems to per-
meate entire regions of my body. An internal engine roars, ceaselessly pulsating, and a choir of voices gathering to a crescendo sings, "You are leaving

China forever, you are actually leaving, you are . . ." It amazes me that no one else seems to hear the song and no one pays any attention to me. The song is so rich and enticing that I totally forget that my mother and I are leaving my father behind, with no idea at all if he will ever rejoin us in America. A spot on his lung led the American Embassy to put him on the Not Wanted list. He was told to wait until the spot disappears and he is clean enough to be admitted. I know he is standing at the end of the wharf, shrouded in mist, his spot still burning inside him. He is leaning gracefully with one hand on his malacca cane, the other rhythmically drawing his cigarette in and out of his mouth. I try not to see him and to concentrate on the excitement within me, an excitement beyond thrill, beyond ferment and flutter, a gargantuan flame. I have been waiting for this moment for years.

A shudder runs through the crowd. Faces turn toward the LST. Its huge door slowly opens, exposing a cavernous, dark interior. The door is lowered and rests on the water, creating a bridge between the wharf and the LST. There is a huge splash as it touches the water. Now we can walk into its yawning hole. The young Marines leap into action, wander through the crowd, give instructions, help carry suitcases.

I march in with my mother behind me and am soon lost in a crowd of people. I know my father is standing on the wharf, somewhere in the mist, and perhaps he is crying. I don't look back. I look forward into the bowels of the massive ship, which is swallowing us whole like the passengers on Noah's Ark. I don't look back. I dream of a bright California sunshine and the sparkle of the Golden Gate.

The Hero of April 8-9

IN MY BOOK my father became a hero on April 8–9, 1949, in Tientsin, a seaport in North China. He did not perform a striking feat of courage or save anyone against great odds, nor was he magnificently noble in a desperate act. During those two days, he stood still and allowed himself to flow with events around him. In that time, the forces of history, the casual kindness of strangers, the strong personality of Mr. George, the Swiss consul in Tientsin, and the dedication of Tsui, a rickshaw "boy," converged on my father, making him the central figure in the drama.

Ordinarily, my father is timid, emotional, easily frightened, romantic, scared of doctors and dentists—and great fun at parties, where he is usually found playing the piano with vigor and enthusiasm, if not always with accuracy. He is not of heroic proportions, but in those two April days I'm convinced he became a hero.

In early 1949 Tientsin was a ghost city, empty of most of its foreign population, who had left the year before when they realized a new regime was moving in. Now it nervously awaited its Communist rulers. European-style office buildings of marble and white stone were turning gray because of the lack of coolie labor to keep them clean. At first glance this area of Tientsin could have been any bourgeois European city, for there were few signs of "chinoiserie" around. But only a few miles away, the Chinese city teemed with alleyways, squalid and colorful outdoor markets, open sewage

In the Forbidden City.

canals, and balconies overflowing with people. Two hours distant were Peking's Forbidden City and the Great Wall of China.

When my father needed an official paper for any purpose, he would go to the Tientsin Hebrew Association to get it. While the English bureaucracy of Tientsin was housed in magnificent Gordon Hall, a castlelike structure in Victoria Park, and the French in an elegant building in the French concession, the Jewish organization's offices were on the second floor of a musty building, clearly indicating our low status on the international totem pole.

At the time of my father's remarkable experience, when the days were showing early signs of spring, though mornings were still winter-crisp, China was in chaos. There was little traffic in the streets. The powerhouse managers had disappeared or been shot by marauding Communist cadres—and as a result there were no streetlights and people were using candles at home. There had been no water for several weeks.

With supervisory staffs gone, Tientsin's civil service system was barely limping along. It had always been permeated with graft and bribes, and now those in charge alternated between uninterested torpor and meaningless meticulousness. People were ignored, requests casually denied, documents lost, and decisions made arbitrarily or not at all.

For months, my father had been making the rounds among the remaining agencies, hoping to find the right person or office to issue him an exit visa, but neither he nor Mr. George—who was trying to help him— had had any success. This had been going on since November 1948, when my mother and I took a U.S. naval ship to Tsingtao, where we boarded the SS *General Butler* for San Francisco. A spot discovered on one of my father's lungs had made him an "undesirable alien" for the Americans, and he was denied a visa.

Since that November day, my father, a Russian Jewish displaced person, had been living with my Aunt Mary and her husband and her father-in-law. He slept on a camp bed behind a blanket strung across a rope nailed to the walls. His two suitcases, carefully packed and ready, were under the bed. Three feet away, the old man slept on a big red-velvet couch and often snored and coughed, keeping my father awake. An ex-cavalry man in the Russian army, the old man often wore his uniform on important occasions. Now shiny and threadbare, bearing golden epaulets, it hung on a thin steel hanger at the foot of the couch.

The dining table in the corner of the room was always set. Covered with a white lace tablecloth, it held four permanent settings and a sparkling crystal bowl—a wedding present to Aunt Mary and her husband—in the center. In the old days, the bowl had been filled with fruit—juicy winter pears, plump cherries, oranges from far-off Florida—but now it was empty.

Every day after she left her office job, Aunt Mary stood in queues, hoping to buy fruit or vegetables for the little family, but both commodities had become increasingly difficult to find. Their servant Soo (or "Boika," as we called him—a Russification of "boy") stood in lines daily for whatever poultry or fish was available, but these too were scarce. Meat had not been seen for months. The market on the corner of Cousins and Davenport Streets, with its curved glass ceiling, was empty. In the old days its stalls had been filled with fresh produce, chickens in cages ready to be decapitated, and fish in tanks of water awaiting their demise; hot sweet potatoes, baked over burning coals in charcoal braziers, had been sold outside in the winter.

The men in the household kept their eyes peeled for whatever buys they might find. Rumors abounded about meat to be had in the German concession, or damp but drinkable tea at Jardine Mathieson's warehouse. One of my father's great achievements that April was finding a whole pound of sugar for sale. Though it was damp and mixed with sand, and Boika had to sift it in the courtyard in the old metal sifter my father had brought from our household, it was good to taste sugar and not have to use boiled-down sweet potatoes for sweetener.

Water was stored in the bathtub and in every available utensil. Tureens, old chamber pots, bottles, dainty crystal decanters on filigreed silver stands, and cloisonné flower vases were filled with the precious fluid, which was used and reused until finally it was doled out to the remaining plants. When the water level in the utensils got alarmingly low, Soo somehow managed to find more; no one ever asked where he got it. There was much talk of stealing water, and it was better not to ask.

The household still had a settled routine. Aunt Mary and my father went to their offices daily, though businesses had virtually ground to a halt. My uncle went out and tried to make deals, but there were few things to buy or sell. He had been a *commerçant*, an entrepreneur, moving skillfully with the times, buying cheap and selling dear—Chinese sables, plump walnuts, hand-carved ivory trinkets, ammunition, jade earrings—whatever was on the market. Now the streets were silent, but he continued to make the rounds of the cafes and offices. The old man napped, or coughed, or sat in the park. Occasionally, he put on his uniform and shined his epaulets and medals. Boika cooked and washed dishes, foraged for food, stole water when necessary, swept the flat, and disappeared at times to visit his wife and children in the Chinese city. My father waited daily to hear when and if he would finally leave China.

On the morning of April 8, my father rose early to take his turn in the one bathroom. The water level in the bathtub was very low; he would have to forgo shaving. Boika served him his breakfast—one scrambled egg, a Chinese *godze*, or fried doughnut, and tea. He walked out into the cool April morning. The mimosas were still in bloom, giving off a musty smell. The streets were deserted as he walked briskly from rue St. Louis to Marchand Avenue, past the imposing, colonnaded, now-deserted Bank of England and Banque de France on Victoria Road and the open-air market on Davenport Road to the Swiss Consulate. He bypassed Victoria Park—too many memories.

In bygone years, when he had strolled through the park, the two red-roofed pagodas had gleamed in the sunset, blinding his vision. The Russian nannies and Chinese amahs had guarded their young European charges, cautioning them to stay clean and out of the sandboxes. Now the place was deserted, its flower beds filled with weeds and the paint on the pagoda roofs starting to peel.

The consulate office on the second floor—the only one doing business in that building—had high ceilings, huge bay windows, and dark-brown mahogany desks. My father had worked for Mr. George, the Swiss consul, for fifteen years, but they still addressed each other by their last names, and they knew little about each other's private lives.

Mr. George and his assistant, Miss Sorenson, were already there when my father came in. Both were tall, angular and spare, and always dressed in dark colors. It was quiet there; the phone seldom rang.

Mr. George had been awaiting instructions to close the consulate. Meanwhile, it was to be business as usual, and the remaining office staff was expected to look busy. For the previous two weeks, the mood in the office had been dark and oppressive. The tea water was brackish. Miss Sorenson's typing contained many mistakes. Mr. George occasionally seemed restless, a strange condition for his usually well-defined, controlled body.

Wang, the office boy, brought in the morning tea, apologizing for the water. Mr. George looked past him as if not hearing the apology and walked into his private office, closing the door. Through the frosted glass, my father could see him slowly pacing. Miss Sorenson kept typing and throwing the papers into the wastebasket. My father filed and refiled dossiers on people long gone; it gave him something to do. The flutter of the twisted papers plopping into the wastebasket, Miss Sorenson's occasional sigh, and Mr. George's soft pacing behind the door were the only sounds.

The offices next door were empty. Highland Brothers Casing Company and Weingarten Novelties, formerly flourishing companies, had closed months before. Their neatly stacked crates lined the hallway, Weingarten's marked FRAGILE on all four sides and addressed to Melbourne, Australia, and the long brown Highland Brothers boxes destined for Pasadena,

California. Unstamped, unclaimed, and forgotten, they had been lying in the hallway for months.

At twelve o'clock my father went to lunch. Outside, Tsui, our rickshaw boy, waited as usual to take him home. The lunch hour was always from twelve to one. While there was no reason to maintain the strict schedule, Mr. George insisted on keeping established routines. He believed that if routines went on, so would civilized life.

Though Tsui was no longer "our" rickshaw boy, as in the old days when he took me to and from school and my mother to the club—and though he could and did take other fares—he always came to the consulate promptly at noon. Tsui and my father had known each other for years, and now both seemed to cling to their relationship as the world they had known crumbled around them. My father knew little of Tsui's private life, other than that he had a wife and two children, who lived with him in our basement. We had seldom seen the family, except at Christmas when they all appeared to get their annual gifts. But Tsui, through his kitchen connections, must have known a lot about us. I don't remember ever having had a conversation with him, other than to tell him where to take me.

After my father stepped into the rickshaw, Tsui picked up the handles in his lean, muscular arms, and swiftly ran to the apartment on rue St. Louis. Into my father's consciousness floated thoughts of his possible exile in China and his aloneness there. Was it possible he would remain forever in this still alien land, where he had come not by choice but as a result of historical circumstances? My father could hear Tsui's regular panting and wheezing, carrying him, as he had done for years, in the rickshaw carriage.

When they stopped in front of the house, my father, tears streaming down his cheeks, stepped out and told Tsui that he was his only friend in China. What must Tsui have thought! He had worked for us for years, living silently with his family in our dank, dark basement—for which, I was always told, he was "grateful," because most other employers did not provide housing. He had transported all of us in his rickshaw through the summer *fu-tiens* with sweat pouring down his back and a wet towel wrapped ineffectively around his neck, and through the winter snowdrifts when I sat in the quilted tent behind him. Tsui, the illiterate, wily peasant, now about to be liberated by his fellow countrymen, grasped my father's hand, stifled a sob, and furiously blew his nose.

My father had some tea and bread for lunch; there was little else and he was not hungry. The old man was napping on the couch, coughing and wheezing as always. Later, he would die of tuberculosis. No one else was at home. My father wanted a second cup of tea, but they were running short of water. He felt depressed and returned to the office before one o'clock, more comfortable there than at home.

The slow afternoon began to unfold. A few pieces of mail had been brought in by Wang, but there was none for my father. Mr. George had nothing in his mail concerning my father. He had been trying for months to expedite my father's planned move to America under the auspices of the Swiss Embassy and the International Red Cross, but neither these efforts nor personal contacts with the new bureaucrats had produced any results. The old, comfortable, well-oiled channels of communication and favors had broken down. In the years when Mr. George was well known in the international and Chinese communities, businesses were smoothly and ritually conducted. How now to communicate with harsh, disinterested, and illiterate bureaucrats who didn't even know him? The afternoon sun came in faintly through the dirt-streaked windows. Everyone drank the brackish tea, and nobody knew where Wang was getting the water.

At 2:34 in the afternoon my father's quiet world was shaken by an enormous explosion. He knew, or thought he knew, it was a bomb, but he couldn't tell where it had landed. Mr. George, Miss Sorenson, and my father rushed to the windows. There was absolutely no activity outside; a hush seemed to have fallen on the streets. It was as if the city were holding its breath, waiting for the next bang. No further explosions came. Mr. George and my father assumed that the Chinese Communists had thrown the bomb into the Russian concession far from the con- sulate—a false but comforting assumption. (The Russian concession, across the Hai-ho Canal, had a huge park filled with giant sycamore trees. We used to go there in a small boat that took off on an irregular sched- ule from a small quay on Victoria Road. There, during the summer, while waiting for the boat, we would buy cardboard containers filled with *prostokvasha*, a delicious, creamy, yogurtlike food, the taste of which I can still conjure up on my tongue.)

They waited, but there were no more loud noises. Mr. George decided to dismiss my father and Miss Sorenson for the day and asked my father to escort her to her home, where she lived with her widowed mother. The two of them walked silently along the deserted streets and parted quickly in front of her flat. He was never to see her again.

That evening the household sat down to a meager meal. Talk was mainly about if and when my father would leave Tientsin to be reunited with my mother and myself. With the explosion of the bomb, it was clear that Communist forces were only days or hours away. Aunt Mary was cheerful and comforting; she was sure things would work out in the end. The old man was quiet, jealous of my father's plans, but not wanting to squelch hope. My uncle was preoccupied with a deal he might be able to make the next day. Tsui carefully measured out a cup of water from the bathtub for the dishes and unobtrusively washed them. Later, he went into the courtyard, where he squatted on the curb, chain-smoking and talking to the other "boys."

Everyone went to bed early. They were saving candles, and besides, the household was exhausted by the day's events. The old man coughed all night and my father could not sleep. He got up with the sun. There was no one in the courtyard. The servants who usually gathered there before their employers awoke were not yet out. He felt as if the city were truly deserted.

Still there had been no further blasts, but everything and everyone seemed to be waiting. A huge weeping willow tree stood in the middle of the courtyard; the bed of flowers surrounding it was dry. The strange, dissonant sounds of a Chinese violin could be heard in the distance.

He arrived at work early, before Mr. George did. Miss Sorenson's desk was very neat; somehow she must have, by habit, tidied it up before she'd left the office. When Mr. George arrived, he looked ruffled; his usually immaculate suit was crumpled and he wore no tie. He stood in the middle of the room without saying a word while my father busied himself shuffling papers and emptying the already empty wastebasket. Then he looked directly at my father, and in a passionless, staccato voice told him that a passage out of Tientsin had been arranged for that day, that he must go and pack immediately, that later that night he was to board the SS *William Tell* to go to the United States. "This has to be done today," he kept repeating. "Today, and you have to hurry."

As my father tells it, his only thought at this announcement was to follow Mr. George's order. My father had always obediently and faithfully followed Mr. George's directions. He would do so now. As he was leaving, Mr. George added that Tsui would first take my father to rue St. Louis, then to see a Mr. Ma in the Chinese city. Mr. Ma was to give my father the final stamp on the pink exit visa, and then Tsui was to deliver him to an Englishman named Mr. Wilson. Mr. Wilson would take him to the SS *William Tell* at Taku Bar, where oceangoing liners berthed, since the Hai-ho Canal was too shallow for big ships. How and when Mr. George had made these elaborate arrangements is unknown to this day.

Tsui was waiting in front of the consulate with his rickshaw as my father came out. My father must have been in a daze, for he had forgotten to thank Mr. George or to say good-bye. Something drew his eye to the bay windows, and he saw Mr. George standing there silently. My father waved but got no response.

When he arrived at the apartment, no one was there. The table was set as usual with four settings. His two suitcases were packed as they had been since December. (There was a saying in Tientsin that we all "lived on our suitcases," meaning we had never put down roots in this foreign land. But we did in spite of ourselves, fragile and transitory roots that have continued to haunt many of us as we settled elsewhere.)

My father completed his packing in twenty minutes, took one last look around, and went downstairs. Tsui was squatting by his rickshaw eating his Chinese doughnut, but seeing my father come out so soon, he hesitated, then threw it into the gutter—a curious act for one who was always hungry. He hurried my father into the rickshaw, tied the two suitcases behind it with ropes, picked up the long handles, and started running.

Everywhere lay an expectant hush. The streets of the French concession were almost empty. They crossed the sturdy Italian bridge to the Chinese part of town. Beyond the bridge, people milled around, groups gathered, talk was loud. Tsui wound his way through the narrow, dirty streets and alleyways where pungent, sulfuric sewage was piling up. Nimbly and gracefully, he avoided the potholes in the street. My father perched tensely in the rickshaw, glancing behind now and then to make sure his suitcases were still there.

Tsui stopped at a grimy four-story building, parked the rickshaw, and motioned my father inside. My father entered a huge chamber with enormous windows that had jagged, broken panes. Some of the broken glass was held together with black tape; newspapers were pasted over other pieces. The once elegant parquet floors were dusty and grimy. There was a generalized din, but through it all one heard the clacking of an abacus and the nasal tones of North Chinese voices.

Elbowing his way through the throng, my father found a place at the counter and presented his letter from Mr. George to Mr. Ma. He was casually waved to a row of chairs. He was the only white man in the room. All the others were well-dressed Chinese seeking favors. They exchanged gossip and paid no attention to my father. An hour passed. The man at the counter was making phone calls, clicking his abacus and picking his teeth. Occasionally, he looked at the row of waiting people, never making eye contact with anyone. His glance was sweeping, disinterested and bored.

The clock on the wall had stopped at 2:37, but, looking down at his neighbor's watch, my father saw that an hour had passed. The counter attendant disappeared behind a bamboo screen; peals of laughter came from behind it. When my father could no longer tolerate the hardness of the chair, he gingerly and hopefully approached the counter. Another man there told him that Mr. Ma had left an hour earlier and would not be back that day. My father was to return the next day. In a quiet, desperate voice, my father told the man he had to be seen that day. The official, bored, irritated, probably impressed with his new power and eager to see the white man desperate, carefully took out a toothpick and stuck it between two gold front teeth. He stared at a point on the ceiling high above my father's head as if in deep concentration. A long time passed while my father propped himself against the soiled wooden counter; by now his knees were shaking and he had broken out in perspiration. Finally, the man glanced at him, wiped some dust from the counter and told him to go to room 212.

Room 212 was on the third floor. It was a small room, much like a dentist's waiting room; old copies of *National Geographic* and a tattered Montgomery Ward catalog dated Spring 1936 lay on a low table. No one was there. Eventually a young woman appeared and took Mr. George's letter to Mr. Ma into an adjoining room. Before my father had a chance to become anxious, she returned with a pink exit visa, encrusted with garish seals and numerous flamboyant signatures. There had been no questions, no conversation, and hardly any waiting. She walked away before my father could thank her.

Outside it was dusk. The smell of burning candles and sewage mingled with the soft evening air. Wash flapped, strung on lines between buildings. Children defecated and urinated in the gutter. Sitting on their balconies, people scooped up rice; their chopsticks made a clicking sound on the bowls. Tsui was waiting outside the building, protectively close to the rickshaw, squatting on his haunches and eating his bowl of rice. They exchanged glances as my father stepped into the rickshaw, and Tsui knew the business had been transacted.

Tsui strode powerfully out of the Chinese district back to Victoria Road. He knew he had to move fast to get my father to his next destination on time. My father, Tsui, and the rickshaw moved like a unit, speeding purposefully to execute the plan laid out earlier. Moving along Victoria Road, my father remembered how the tall, majestic-looking Sikhs in their uniforms used to guard the British Bank in eight-hour shifts.

They stopped at the Elgin Building. My father does not remember if he said good-bye to Tsui. They may have exchanged glances. There were no extraneous movements that night. Tsui disappeared around the corner.

The Elgin Building—once the most elegant office building in Tientsin, its eleven stories making it the highest in the city—was almost empty. Only two windows were dully lit. The elevator was not working, so my father walked up six flights of stairs to the offices of the now defunct American Embassy. Mr. Wilson, a tall, ruddy Englishman whom my father had never seen before, was waiting.

Wilson welcomed my father with "Mr. George sent you, right? It's going to take a bit of doing to get you out, you know." Once, as the evening wore on, he asked my father if he would like a "spot of rum." Other than that, there was no conversation.

Mr. Wilson napped and took regular shots of rum from a bottle. My father leafed through old *Life* magazines. He realized he had not left a message at home to let the family know he was leaving, and there was no way to do it now, since they had no phone. He hoped they would realize what had happened when they missed the suitcases.

At eight o'clock Mr. Wilson suddenly jumped up and said, "We're ready. Let's go." They walked down the stairs, which were only dimly lit and in places in total darkness. Outside the entrance stood an American Jeep, driven by a man with a French accent who said he was Mr. Duchamp. He too was unknown to my father.

They drove to the Bund, the area paralleling the canal. Once it had been a busy warehouse center, where cargo was put on small vessels and later loaded on ocean liners. Now it was deserted. Duchamp switched off the Jeep's lights and my father was able by the light of the new moon to make out a group of men, apparently waiting for Mr. Wilson. Heaving his bulk out of the Jeep, Mr. Wilson turned to my father and said, "These are the stevedores who will be loading cargo on the *William Tell.* You will go with them."

They were young White Russians, burly and powerful, each carrying a bottle of vodka. Though they were full of high spirits, foulmouthed and crude, none remarked on my father and his two suitcases. It was as if that day everyone conspired to pass him from place to place without comment.

Mr. Wilson waved my father to an empty warehouse that looked ghostly and deserted. A sign reading "Jardine Mathieson" was still hanging across the front, reminding my father that this had once been a large shipping company, a giant in the industrial world. He could barely make out the huge, neatly stacked crates, but later, snapping his cigarette lighter on, he saw that they were destined for Mexico and the United States. There was no way to tell what was inside them.

Sitting on a crate marked "Pasadena, California," my father could see the Hai-ho Canal and hear an occasional "plop" as a small boat rubbed against its moorings. He recalled the times he'd carried me piggyback along this very road when I got tired, far from the main street. He sat with his two suitcases and waited. He told me it occurred to him then that Mr. Wilson might possibly never come back, or that the Russian stevedores could, as a drunken joke, take off without him.

Time passed. He dozed. He smoked cigarette after cigarette, snuffing out the butts carefully and arranging them in a pile. Suddenly Mr. Wilson appeared and said, "Time to go." My father followed the tall Englishman out of the warehouse to the pier, where a barge was waiting. The stevedores, now quite drunk, kidded about the Yid, poked each other gleefully, and told elaborate anti-Semitic jokes. They eyed my father and exploded into raucous adolescent laughter.

Out of the dark appeared a Chinese official, carrying a notebook with "Property of the U.S. Government" printed on the cover. Perhaps he had been employed at the American Embassy and had "confiscated" it. The laughter diminished. The official demanded papers, and Mr. Wilson, puffing on his cheroot, slowly produced a group identification card for the stevedores.

Squinting suspiciously at my father, the official said, "That one can't board; he's not with the group." Mr. Wilson produced my father's pink exit paper, but the other man was not impressed. The Russians squatted and continued their drinking, but the encounter had sobered them and they no longer laughed. Mr. Wilson puffed on his pipe and produced another document, but that too was brushed aside.

Mr. Wilson and the official walked away from the group, and from a distance their voices—Mr. Wilson's sonorous, even-tempered one and the official's shrill, angry one—could be heard for at least twenty minutes. My father waited patiently, smoking endless cigarettes and stacking the butts in piles. Finally, Mr. Wilson walked up to him and said, "Go right now." The Russians jumped up, their energy recharged, and burst into song. Mr. Wilson turned and disappeared into the misty night.

A few stars could be seen, and the sliver of new moon provided a weak spot of light. The barge's engines purred as they started up to head toward the SS *William Tell*. As the Hai-ho began to widen, pushing toward the open sea, my father strained his eyes to find the ship. The darkness and the mist fogging his eyeglasses made it impossible for him to discern clear shapes. He didn't ask the Russians if they could see the ship; they were too drunk to give him a serious answer. He felt alone on the barge, facing the open sea.

Soon the engines came to a stop, and the waves swooshed against the sides of the barge. There was no ship in sight. The barge swayed back and forth in the water. Birds flew across the moon, pasting dark shadows on its whiteness. It was cold and my father wanted to get his overcoat from a suitcase, but it was lying at the other end and he did not want to try to walk across the swaying barge. They waited.

Finally, the prow of a ship appeared around the bend. It loomed ahead, gray and powerful, about a third of a mile away. The Russians, realizing their night's work lay ahead, began to get ready.

When the barge came parallel to the broad gray hulk of the SS *William Tell,* my father's heart sank as he looked up at the impenetrable gray wall that he was to climb. Given to spells of dizziness and fear of heights, he now raged at the thought that he might not be able to meet the final challenge. Several sailors were leaning on the deck's rail, looking down at the swaying barge. He could hear their clipped British voices and occasional laughter.

A thin steel ladder was lowered. It swayed from side to side. A dark-haired stevedore caught it and, turning to my father, pushed his U.S. Marine cap back, smacked his thigh, and said in a loud, drunken voice, "Well, Yid, up to freedom." Before my father had time to think, he was on the third rung, with the Russians yelling insults and coarse encouragement.

Rung by rung he crept up the ladder, drenched with fear and the desire to succeed and egged on by the jibes below. About halfway up the steel mountain he stopped, but a hand smacked him brusquely on his buttocks and shoved him forward. As he stepped over the ship's railing to the deck, he realized that the man had been behind him, carrying his two suitcases. They were now flung onto the deck—and without a word the stevedore disappeared down the ladder. Looking down, my father saw him pick up a box, which he hoisted on his shoulder, and then he scampered up the ladder again. The other stevedores sang loud Russian songs as the tempo of their work heightened.

The ship was bursting with activity, English sailors and officers shouting orders to the stevedores. My father, guarding his suitcases, was the only person standing still in this vortex of energy. Nobody paid any attention to him. He felt again as if he were passing almost invisibly through other people's lives, on the way to his own destiny.

Then a young lieutenant in immaculate dress blues came up to him and in his clipped English accent said, "Welcome aboard. I'll take you to your cabin." His blond hair barely showing beneath his slightly oversized, blue-visored cap, he was clean-cut and courteous. Several sailors smartly saluted the lieutenant along the way. He could have been welcoming my father to high tea in an English country house rather than steering him through a poorly lit cargo ship sneaking through the Yellow Sea. My father followed him through narrow corridors to an elegant stateroom. On the table were fresh fruit and a bottle of whiskey.

The spigots in the bathroom gleamed. As he turned one on, clear water burst forth. My father began to cry.

Salute to the Promised Land

"THIS IS THE last time we are fleeing," my father tells me. "The very last. Fleeing two revolutions is more than enough for any man. I've had more than my share. Now we stay put."

Six months after my mother's and my arrival in the United States, we are reunited with my father, who came on the SS *William Tell* first to San Diego and then to San Francisco. We are again a family.

We settle into an apartment at 1831 Van Ness Avenue with Mrs. Bosak, who belongs to the group of Russian Jews that have filtered into San Francisco from China since the end of the war in 1945. Although we come from different towns in China, she welcomes us like long-lost relatives. She has hastily organized one room in her two-room apartment for us, but many of her mementos remain—an orange lacquered box, a headless jade figurine, and photos of her family. We put up our own family photographs, and the ghosts of the Bosak family and my family stare at each other across the room.

We eat together in the cramped kitchen with flowered curtains from Penney's bargain basement. Mrs. Bosak and my mother boil pots of red beet borscht and make mounds of potato salad. Mrs. Bosak recently lost her husband and says we are a godsend to her in her loneliness.

Everything astonishes and pleases me the first few months—the night hum of the gleaming white refrigerator, the wideness of Van Ness Avenue at my doorstep, the cable cars that slide down Powell Street, and

Finally in the Promised Land.

the carousel at Fairyland by the Beach whose wild trajectory makes me
gasp. I savor newfound words like "Murphy bed," "Pullman kitchen,"
"downtown," and "five-and-ten." I discover that a drugstore does more
than sell drugs, and I become a regular customer at Danevi's Pharmacy,
corner of Van Ness and Broadway, brashly ordering sundaes "with everything" on them.

A month later, through a connection in the San Francisco Russian Jewish community, I start work as a typist for Vitkin's Novelty, Inc., which sells Christian religious bric-a-brac. Joseph Vitkin, a Jew, knows our family from China. He came to San Francisco ten years ago and, as he puts it, "fell into the religious bric-a-brac business." Under his guidance, Vitkin's Novelty, Inc., has prospered.

"Vitkin's Novelties—the crappiest religious junk in town," one gum-popping salesman tells me the first day. "Takes a super salesman to sell this crap. But it's a living." He winks at me, puts his hand on my shoulder, and keeps it there. I feel the calluses through my thin blouse and shrug him off. "Okay girly-girl, no harm done," he says and wanders off whistling.

Mr. Vitkin assigns me to a typewriter in the windowless back room facing Drumm Street. That morning, surrounded by boxes marked "VASES, FRAGILE," and squeezed in between two towering office files, I assure myself this will only be a temporary position until things settle down and my father finds work.

One day several salespeople do not show up for work. Mr. Vitkin yells to anyone within earshot, "Americans! They're lazy. Unreliable. Out to have fun. No sense of commitment." Then, seeing me in the corner, he says loudly, "Your father—tell him to come and work for me. I know he's reliable. He's one of us."

At dinner that night I tell my father about Mr. Vitkin's offer. "Selling religious bric a-brac? Door-to-door? What do I know about that?" he says.

"It will be just for a while, until something better comes along," says my mother.

"Who would have thought. Door-to-door. Me, A salesman. A Jew selling Christian religious ornaments. Only in America!"

"We'll be working in the same office," I plead. "And if the job works out for you, maybe I can quit mine. It's a nice office, really." I lie boldly, extravagantly, in order to convince him.

My father hesitates and looks away from me, hunching his shoulders. I know he hates the fact that I am the sole support of the family. He wants me to be a scholar, a writer, a musician, a teacher. Anything but a typist in a dingy back room on Drumm Street. He is so filled with the pain that he cannot talk. Instead he laughs. "Why not? Have to start somewhere in the Promised Land. Salute!" We raise our glasses of orange juice and toast each other.

Mrs. Bosak wipes a tear from her eyes. "My Solomon would have been so happy to see this. A success story. Two people working in one family."

"To Solomon, 'Tsarstvo emu nebestnoye' (May he rest in peace)," my mother says. The two women hug each other tearfully.

"Everything is possible in America," declares my father as he refills our glasses with orange juice.

Next morning we take the Powell cable car to work. My father marvels at the speed and precariousness of the machine, and I reassure him that we will not fall off the tracks. He is like a wide-eyed child, excited, talkative, bursting with energy.

"My daughter here," he brags to the conductor, "is a big shot! A regular employment agency. She got me my first job in this wonderful country, and this is my first day."

The conductor mutters something under his breath, looks bored, and continues shifting his gears. That my father should be satisfied with so little embarrasses me. All I did was to carry the message from Mr. Vitkin. Doesn't he know that his pride in me is misplaced, and that my motives are purely selfish? He continues to boast to the other totally disinterested passengers. I feel sick with shame and am relieved when we finally arrive at the corner of Drumm and Market.

Nightly my father talks about his assigned territory. It is a sprawling housing project called Hunters Point where the paint on the mud-colored, three-story buildings has long ago been peeled away. The inhabitants are mainly black. My father tells us that the area is poorly kept up, that the gutters are unswept, that there are potholes in the middle of the streets. Packs of homeless dogs roam the area. He sells door-to-door, wandering with his suitcases past the dogs and the scraggly pyracantha bushes, past young children playing ball and young boys leaning idly against walls.

"There is garbage everywhere and the corridors are dimly lit and the steps are so slippery that I have to watch my step in order not to fall. But I am grateful to Vitkin for giving me a start. This is just the beginning," my father says.

Every morning he methodically organizes his merchandise, wrapping the plates, ashtrays, and vases carefully in old newspapers. The watches and earrings he wraps in kitchen towels. Everything has a religious motif. Soup bowls have garish Last Supper pictures painted on them. Lamp bases are sculptured into figures of Jesus Christ nailed to the cross, and lamp shades have paintings of the Virgin Mary cradling a baby Jesus. When lit, the baby Jesus looks greenish-white and sickly in the glare. Fake gold crosses dangle from earrings.

"Incredible what people will buy," he says, shaking his head as he fastens his suitcases in preparation for the day. "I sold six soup bowls to one lady yesterday. A dollar down and fifty cents a week for this junk. Sometimes I feel I'm cheating them, but Mr. Vitkin tells me that blacks live in a perpetual fog and cannot really understand their condition. Mr. Vitkin says we're doing them a favor, supplying them with goods to brighten their lives. I don't know. I really don't know. But it's a job. My first job in the Promised Land."

"You'll find something better soon," I promise.

"Of course. No need to worry," he says bravely.

We are interrupted by a car honking outside. It is the senior salesman who comes daily to pick up my father. He hurries out of the apartment, carrying one Jesus lamp under each arm, their bases covered in brown paper bags to protect them from the rain. The senior salesman, the one who winked at me on my first day at the job, does not get out to help my father. He idly smokes a cigarette, his hat tipped to the back of his head, and appears to stare off into space. I watch my father as he scurries around loading his merchandise, the rain dripping from his well-worn fedora. He looks so humble, I think, so servile and meek. A friend once said my father was docile and humble. "Just knuckles under, instead of standing up to things. *My* father would never do that." I remember those words as I stand looking at my father through the rain-spattered windowpane, trying to get his attention. He looks up and I yell, "Get that man to help you." My father looks puzzled. I repeat myself, but he does not hear me. He waves gaily to me as the car roars off. I sit down on the floor and cry.

At dinner my father announces, "There are no men in the projects. All women. Rows and rows of houses, and all women and children."

"The black men come and go," explains Mrs. Bosak. "The whole Negro society is brought up by women."

"There are some boys, but all they do is stand and smoke. Few over fifteen years." My father's voice is puzzled.

"That's the way they are. Solomon always said there is no way to understand a Negro. Some are okay. He knew one that played the violin," Mrs. Bosak says that with awe. "Imagine that. Playing a violin."

"Mr. Vitkin tells me only to sell to the Negroes. There are a few whites and Orientals in the projects, but I have been instructed not to sell to them."

"It's because only the Negroes will buy that *drek*," Mrs. Bosak laughs heartily.

My father's jaw muscles tighten and he purses his lips in a tight line. I know the sign of his anger. His thick eyebrows clench in a V. My mother bustles around the kitchen, noisily ladling soup into our already over-flowing soup bowls, humming under her breath.

"I'm starting a new class at night school," I interject, trying desperately to diffuse the thick tension that grips my throat like a vice.

"Fine. Fine," my father mutters, his fists clenched.

"Wonderful. What is it?" my mother asks with forced cheeriness.

Before I have time to answer, my father throws his napkin on the floor and leaves the room, slamming the door behind him. It is quiet except for the sounds of the radio next door.

"Americans! Always surrounded by noise. All night long. Don't they ever sleep?" comments Mrs. Bosak. Then turning to me, she says, "Eat. Eat. Everything will work out. You'll see. He'll get used to this new life."

My mother and I exchange glances. We know how he hates his demeaning job, how he hates preying on the poor. As Mrs. Bosak dashes briskly about the kitchen, she seems totally unaware that she has triggered my father's rage. I feel a familiar pain, close to my heart, the size of a mountain, and I breathe with difficulty. It explodes, twinlike to my father's pain. I do not fully understand his but can feel mine, and I have never told this to anyone in the whole world. I wait until it subsides and I can breathe again.

One day my father tells us that a dog chased him up three flights of unlit stairs and he was finally saved from the beast by a woman who opened her door and let him in.

"Then she bought a pair of vases. The ugliest things I've ever seen. I hate selling them, but Mr. Vitkin tells me he knows what appeals to the heart of a Negro."

"He should. He's been here for at least ten years," my mother's voice is brisk.

"And he's made that whole business of his grow. Started from nothing. My Solomon was his very first salesman." Mrs. Bosak fingers a napkin, dabs at her eyes.

"Tsarstvo emu nebestnoye," whispers my mother as she glances at the enlarged photograph on the wall of Solomon Bosak.

"Still, I hate selling things I don't believe in," my father persists.

"This is America. And in America business is what counts. No one is asking how you feel and what you believe in. What counts is how you sell." Mrs. Bosak focuses her beady eyes on my father, her upper lip wet with perspiration as she earnestly tries to convince him.

"That's what the salespeople of Mr. Vitkin tell me. Sell and don't think. But not only am I selling shoddy and ugly merchandise, I'm selling it to people who cannot afford it."

"So who are you to know what they can and cannot afford?"

"And can we afford not to eat?" my mother mutters in a strained voice as she bustles around the kitchen cleaning a spotless counter and nervously rearranging cookies in a jar. She is close to tears, and I realize for the first time the weight of her terror at the thought of my father's being out of work, just as Mrs. Bosak fears her roomers won't pay their rent. Our entire existence hangs on my father's ability to sell Jesus lamps. The fears are unspoken, but the panic in the room is so vibrant it suffocates me. I need to escape.

"Not hungry tonight, got to rush to class," I mumble as I hurry out into the street, thankful it is Monday and the beginning of my new English literature class. I run out without a coat, and the chilly night air stuns me. I hesitate, but rather than go back to the steamy room I walk briskly on, relishing the coolness against my skin and relieved at leaving the problems behind me. The farther I am from 1831 Van Ness Avenue, the lighter I feel. I begin to run, my feet seeming not to touch the sidewalk, and I feel I am floating above the rooftops and see the whole world spread out before me. I sing to myself over and over, "I will not be at Vitkin Novelties forever."

Hope knocks my breath away and I explode with imaginary special powers. My father will get a magnificent job. I will write. We will live in a mansion. I will compose. Create. The world is mine. I embrace an elm tree, rubbing my face against its grainy bark, and feel feverish.

Several weeks later my father brings home a sweet potato pie. It is still warm and covered with tinfoil.

"The blacks all eat sweet potato pie," announces Mrs. Bosak. "It is their favorite food."

"From Mrs. Beasley," says my father. I spoon out a bite and roll the unfamiliar creamy concoction in my mouth.

"Why the pie?" my mother questions. "This is the third pie you've bought. Last week it was coconut. I thought all the Negroes are poor."

"Mrs. Beasley *is* poor." My father's voice is defensive.

"Is she paying her weekly amount? A dollar down and fifty cents a week?"

My father doesn't answer and looks away. He disappears right in front of me, just as he always does when he doesn't want to face things.

"Remember you only get commission when they pay up. If they don't pay, you don't get it. And if you don't get a commission, we don't eat. She's bribing you with pies. It's the *payment* you want."

"I'm getting my commission," my father hisses through clenched teeth. "The subject is closed."

He storms out of the room. I run after him.

"Pa. It's all right. I'll stay on at Vitkin's. I don't mind the typing."

He doesn't turn around, but stands still. "Don't argue with me, young lady. You'll be out of there soon. Soon."

Slowly he walks away from me into the bathroom. The door slams, the dishes in the kitchen cupboard rattle.

One rainy day I come home after work, and as I climb the musty staircase, noticing the frayed carpeting, I hear loud voices coming from our apartment. There is an argument going on. My first instinct is to flee.

"How can you quit now?" my mother's voice sounds tearful.

"I can't go on." His words are slow coming.

"He'll find another job. He has to!" Mrs. Bosak's voice is struggling to be convincing.

I walk into the kitchen. "*Sha*, hush," says my mother as she sees me come in. Mrs. Bosak motions me toward the already set table and we eat in silence. I hold back my tears and wonder if I should have turned around on the stairway and fled. My father must be quitting his job, and my worst nightmare is coming true. Forever doomed to Drumm Street, I think to myself, typing price lists of ceramic Jesus lamps and fake gold earrings.

"Cheer up," my father's voice sifts through my reverie.

"What happened? Are you quitting?"

"I got electrocuted," he says, not answering my question.

"What?"

"Electrocuted! The final insult. I got electrocuted by a defective wiring when I tried to plug in the Jesus lamp in Mrs. Carter's apartment."

"Are you all right?"

"I'm fine. But I said to myself after I got out of the apartment, 'What is a Jewish intellectual from China doing getting electrocuted selling shoddy, defective Jesus lamps in an all-black neighborhood, where the only inhabitants are women, children, and vicious dogs?' "

The imagery is so ludicrous that I burst out laughing. I can't stop laughing. Water gushes out of my eyes. My father looks at me and joins my laughter. My mother smiles. Mrs. Bosak folds her arms on her ample bosom. Rocking back and forth, she keeps repeating, "Solomon would have loved this. Solomon should be here. 'Electrocuted!' " Her laughter changes into tears, and my mother stands up, puts her arms around her, and says, "Tsarstvo emu nebestnoye."

My limbs go weak with relief. The laughter has dispelled the gloom and the room feels lighter. The rain has stopped and the green poplar tree leaves look fresh and dewy. Mrs. Bosak turns off the light and the kitchen is bathed in soft afternoon sunshine.

"It's been getting more and more ridiculous," my father continues. "I haven't been telling you all. First of all, Mrs. Beasley has not been able to pay her weekly amounts, and—you were right—she has been trying to pay me off with sweet potato pies. She was doing the best she could, but she's got serious problems at home. Her sixteen-year-old daughter got pregnant and her nine-year-old is in the hospital with polio."

"So, you've been paying her weekly amount," my mother says, shaking her head in disbelief.

"Yes. So I could get my commission."

"Something is wrong in that arithmetic."

My father ignores the remarks. "Well, anyway, after Mrs. Beasley stopped paying, Mrs. Howe became irregular in her payments and pleaded with me not to take away her Jesus lamp. Then there were the dogs that kept after me. They run loose all over the project and don't belong to anyone. So I started buying dog biscuits to bribe them, and that began to cost quite a penny."

"You were supporting the entire community," Mrs. Bosak screams hysterically.

"Right. So yesterday when I tried to plug in the lamp to show Mrs. Carter how it works and I got a jolt, I said to myself, 'This is enough! Surely the Promised Land has something better to offer.'"

"Something will come along," says Mrs. Bosak. "I'll call my friend Herb Rottenberg tomorrow. He knows a roofer who needs a salesman. Why didn't I think of this before? He sells good-quality material. And nothing religious about roofs," she snickers.

"Yes, call him tomorrow." My mother's voice is full of hope.

"Why not now? No need to wait. Solomon always said, 'Never wait for tomorrow.'" Mrs. Bosak eases her ample body out of her chair and waddles toward the hall to phone. We hear her dialing.

My mother gets up to bring more soup. The stuffed cabbage rolls sizzle gently in their juice behind me on the stove. From the hallway we hear Mrs. Bosak's muffled voice making connections to our future.

"Salute! To the Promised Land!" my father says, lifting his cup of orange juice.

We join the toast. "To the Promised Land."

Singular Lives